For Anne Eileen

Poppies and Roses

A Story of Courage

MARJORIE SELDON

First published in 1985

by

Economic and Literary Books
PO Box 193, Sevenoaks,
Kent TN15 0JW

© ECONOMIC & LITERARY BOOKS 1985

British Library Cataloguing in Publication Data

Seldon, Marjorie
Poppies and roses: story of courage.
1. Willett (*Family*)   2. Kent – Genealogy
I. Title
929'.2'0942   CS439.W5

ISBN 0-948115-00-9

Printed in England by

GORON PRO-PRINT CO LTD

6 Marlborough Road, Churchill Industrial Estate, Lancing, W. Sussex

Filmset 'Berthold' 11 on 13pt Baskerville

Contents

Illustrations

vi

NOTES ON ILLUSTRATIONS

Front cover: *The Rosery, Wilfred, Eileen.*

Back cover: *The author in The Rosery garden, 1923.*

Between pages 26 and 27:

Mrs Seager, Wilfred's grandmother, about 1860.
Wilfred's father, Thomas, at Tintagel, 1911.
Wilfred's mother, Susie, at Tintagel, 1911.

William Willett, Wilfred's uncle, founder of Daylight Saving (Summer Time), about 1914.
A page from his pamphlet on the Daylight Saving Bill, 1908.
His Petrol-Air-Light Generator, 1914.

Wilfred with Kate, Tintagel, 1911.
Wilfred at Cambridge, 1910.
Wilfred with friends at St Paul's School, 1908.

Wilfred with the Trinity College Rifle Club team, 1911.
The Trinity Rugger Boat, 1911.

Wilfred and Susie at Military Tournament, Cambridge, O.T.C., 1911.
May Week, 1911.

Wilfred with O.T.C. friends, 1910.
Wilfred with Floss, Wisborough Green, 1912.
Captain Thornton, Rifle Brigade, Cambridge Degree Day, 1911.

Wilfred at Cambridge O.T.C., Isle of Wight, 1912.

Wilfred and Eileen in 1914.
The Mention in Despatches from Field Marshal Sir John French signed by Winston Churchill.

Between pages 90 and 91:

In The Rosery garden: the thrush's egg, 1922.

The Rosery in 1916.
St Luke's Church and Matfield War Memorial, 1919.
Old Ebenezer and Chapel Row, 1919.

Eileen with Denis, 1918.
Nannie Read with Denis, 1918.
Denis and Marjorie in The Rosery nursery, 1920.

Map of Matfield, with insets of Tunbridge Wells and surrounding Kent countryside.

SOURCES OF ILLUSTRATIONS

The photograph of Eileen on the dust-jacket was taken by Wilfred to France and bears the creases of lying in his pocket book. It was, almost certainly, on him when he was wounded.

The photograph of Wilfred on the dust-jacket was taken from a studio photograph of a 1913 Cambridge University Rugger team.

The early photographs of St Paul's School, Cambridge, Tintagel and army training camps were taken from Wilfred's pre-Great War album.

The 1860 photograph of Mrs Seager was given to me by my father.

The photograph of William Willett was loaned by his grand-daughter, Monica Mason.

The photograph of the Willett Light Generator was lent by Colin Parnham.

The Sassoon photographs were loaned by Major Leo Sassoon.

The photographs of Matfield House, Newbolds' Stores, Matfield Green, and the Ebenezer Chapel are by courtesy of the Brenchley Local History Society.

Early child photographs, including the one of the author on the back of the dust-jacket, were taken by Miss Agnes Tomlinson, sister of the vicar of Matfield, and were assembled, with others of the inter-War years, by Wilfred.

'The Homestead' photograph is by courtesy of the present owners, Mr and Mrs Max Lewis, and Bracketts Estate Agency, Tunbridge Wells.

The pen and ink drawing of St Luke's Church, Matfield, is by E. G. Grenham.

The drawings of birds, including some by Roland Green, on pages 10, 14, 24, 36, 73, 77, 106, 109, 129, 175, 191 are from Wilfred Willett's books British Birds *and* Birds of Britain *by permission of the publishers, A. & C. Black.*

The drawings of flowers by Amy Webb on pages 64 and 186 are from Wilfred Willett's British Wild Flowers and their Garden Varieties *by permission of the publishers, Ward, Lock.*

The sketches by A. H. Patterson are taken from letters to Wilfred.

M.S.

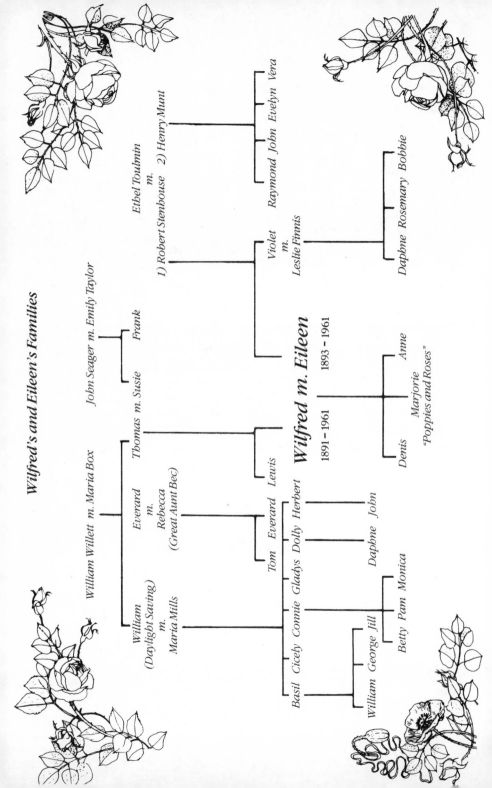

Wilfred's and Eileen's Families

William Willett m. Maria Box

John Seager m. Emily Taylor

Ethel Toulmin
m.
1) Robert Stenhouse   2) Henry Munt

Everard
m.
Rebecca
(Great Aunt Bec)

Thomas m. Susie

Frank

Raymond John Evelyn Vera

William
(Daylight Saving)
m.
Maria Mills

Tom Everard Lewis

Violet
m.
Leslie Finnis

Daphne Rosemary Bobbie

Basil Cicely Connie Gladys Dolly Herbert

Daphne John

Wilfred m. Eileen

1891 – 1961   1893 – 1961

William George Jill

Denis   Marjorie   Anne
"Poppies and Roses"

Betty Pam Monica

Author's Note

The story of my parents' lives in the peaceful years, 1919 to 1939, in the village of Matfield, Kent, would not be complete without the perspective of the Great War. This part of the story was told in the form of a novel, *Wilfred and Eileen*, by Jonathan Smith, which was turned into a radio play and a television series. To his moving reconstruction of their early life, I have been able to add details about the family and the early events which were not appropriate to the novel.

Part I of *Poppies and Roses*, The Beginnings in War, is a brief account of their meeting in Cambridge, their secret marriage, and their courage in 1914 which will give the reader an understanding of their characters and the way in which the war affected them and the children born to them in the peaceful years.

Many of the conversations in Part I and Part II of the book took place and were recorded by my father in unpublished autobiographical material. It would have been difficult to invent what the villagers said to one another at the 1919 parish meeting about the war memorial, what the 'gentry' said at the time of the 1926 General Strike, and what the vicar and Wilfred said to each other, as in disagreement about Lenin and the Russian Revolution. These voices and others of the church ladies, the village welfare committee and many more echoing 'under the arches of the years' enhanced my own memories by glimpses of a vanished world and of attitudes long since forgotten.

My recollections include stories told me by my grandparents, parents, other relatives and by 'Tol', a governess in my maternal grandmother's house who died in Seaford aged 90.

While every practicable effort has been made to ensure accuracy in dates and descriptions of events, many witnesses are no longer living. Any remaining errors or omissions are unintentional and are sincerely regretted.

The idea of writing *Poppies and Roses* (which I first called *The Rosery, Matfield*) arose from the interest in the B.B.C.'s *Wilfred and Eileen*. I had many letters and requests to know 'what happened to them after 1916?' I therefore prepared a draft or synopsis, which did not include picking up the threads of the Great War story nor of its continuation until my parents died in 1961, but was to be an account of 'the peaceful years'. I sent it to the two publishers (hard-back and paper-back) of Jonathan Smith's novel. There was no interest. I was then inclined to abandon the idea of writing a book, but the encouragement of Professor Richard Cobb and of Jonathan Smith persuaded me to go ahead.

I began to enjoy the task of recreating my childhood in telling my parents' story, but my hope that I would see it in print faded as I read well-documented accounts of the difficulties experienced by new authors in getting a book published. It has been said that the market for such work is almost non-existent. Publishers find it difficult enough, so runs the general belief, to make a commercial success out of books by writers who, although they may have their work published, are not nationally known names.

Publishers must be market-orientated. They are not, after all, charities. Yet, as a profession, they are probably short on risk-taking. They are unlikely to be quick to discover that the public taste for explicit sex, brutal violence and mayhem is waning, to be replaced by books that people like to read — an echo of Richard Cobb's description of books chosen for the 1984 Booker Prize short list. Perhaps the growth in the number of middle-aged readers who now have more leisure due to early retirement is significant.

Many people have a story to tell: a good novel to write. But the small prospect of publication discourages them from writing it. *The Writers' and Artists' Yearbook*, in advice which, however well-intentioned, seems a 'closed shop' homily, urges authors not to attempt to publish their own work and asserts (without persuasive evidence and in spite of cases to the contrary) that, if it has any merit it will, sooner or later, find a publisher. This judgement is misleading; it will condemn many writers to fruitless search and dispiriting disappointment. The admonition not to publish themselves ought not to deter them from risking their money in backing their own work, as many could. (Printing costs with binding for 2,000 hardback copies would be around £2 each, more for illustrations, but decreasing per copy for a larger number.)

There are efficient printers who will give technical information and advice on where to find publishing expertise. And there are book distributors specialising in marketing the work of small publishers. If more authors grasped the nettle of do-it-yourself publishing and found it neither so difficult nor as costly as they thought and readers liked their books, conventional publishers would have to become more adventurous in selecting new writing. Authors and readers would benefit from more flexibility in publishing and variety in books published. There would be a quicker response to changing tastes.

Poppies and Roses has not had to go through the hoops of finding a publisher. My husband, Arthur Seldon, after reading the first half of the book, proposed it be published by *E & L Books*.

My first acknowledgement in these pages is to him for his editing, his suggestions for improvements, expansion or curtailment in the text. Although I cannot echo the words of another author who thanked him for his help 'without whom this book would have been twice as long', I now see that, although I demurred at the removal of some of my treasured phrases, the end result is immeasurably better than it would otherwise have been. That it is not perfect in every respect is due to me and not to him.

No less is my gratitude to Richard Cobb and Jonathan Smith. I could not have worked on my early draft without their encouragement. My affection for them goes back many years. I remember how much pleasure Richard's visits to The Rosery gave my father. I remember how kind Jonathan was to my son, Anthony, at Tonbridge. They have both written books which delighted me: Jonathan's *Wilfred and Eileen* with its tender descriptions of my parents' life in 1913 and 1914 and Richard's *Still Life* with its evocative pictures of Tunbridge Wells in the 1920's and 30's. I, too, remember the town well: I was wearing the blue and black badge of the High School when he wore the pink rose of Rose Hill School! To Richard for loving my father and writing a memoir, to Jonathan for his kindness and friendship and for contributing his recollections, I offer very heartfelt thanks.

My sister and I were deeply moved by Alexander Baron's perception of our parents. And I am grateful to him for his ready willingness to read the book in page-proof and give his opinion of it.

I thank Martin Anderson who good-humouredly read the typescript for literary accuracy, John Raybould who advised on marketing, Gordon and Ron of Goron Pro-print, who took immense trouble in reproducing the old photographs, Bob who set the text, and Jeannette Giblin who designed the dust-jacket and felt she should read the typescript before she did so. I thank David Prestage for producing a sketch-map of Matfield that will help readers to follow the story.

Not least my thanks go to Jean Durham who not only typed the MS efficiently but encouraged me by saying, as she received each instalment, that she 'couldn't wait to see what happened next'.

Godden Green,   M.S.
November 1984

Going to See Wilfred

RICHARD COBB

Just getting there was part of the sheer enjoyment provided by each one of those visits to the cottage, half-hidden by the high hedge, between the Green and the War Memorial.

During the War years, every time I was home in Tunbridge Wells for a few days' leave, and in the second half of the 40s and throughout the 50s, each time I was over from Paris or from Aberystwyth, I would ring up Mrs Willett. It would be the first thing I would do once in the house: 'When can I come and see Wilfred?' And she would reply: 'Just hold on while I go and ask him' (and it was as if I could *see* her going through to the marvellous, smoky den on the garden side of the cottage). Then, after a minute or two, she would return to the phone: 'Come to tea tomorrow, he would love to see you; but come after 3.30, he has a visitor till then'.

I was very fond of Mrs Willett. She always treated me rather like a wayward schoolboy, as if she could read all my secrets, even when I was well on in my 30s. I don't think she was very interested in politics, but I do know that she was one of my mother's favourite bridge partners; my mother also greatly admired her courage and her energy. Mrs Willett always greeted me with a smile that hinted at some sort of complicity (in, I suppose, a share, mine only a very small one, in Wilfred): 'Hullo Richard, did you come over on your bike? Wilfred is waiting for you, you know the way'. To me, she was always Mrs Willett; she still is. It was only after Jonathan Smith's book came out that I learnt her Christian name was Eileen. In any case, I would never have thought of calling any of my mother's friends by their Christian names.

It was different with Wilfred; I suppose because he was both ageless and absolutely unique, the one and only Wilfred. He was

Wilfred to quite an amazing range of people: female farm-workers and domestic servants come to consult him about a union, high-ups from the Party (perhaps they called him Comrade Wilfred, but I doubt it) and middle-class young men like me. He was also Wilfred (pronounced Vil*fred*) to two quite devoted French families who lived somewhere down near Limoges and with whom he would stay every now and then.

So getting there was all part of it, offering both the excitement of anticipation and the choice of two or three possible routes. I would nearly always cycle over – though once or twice I may have walked it via the cinder path and High Woods – and my favourite way was through Hawkenbury and the Kipping's Cross road, over the stream, then by the primrose woods, the fringes of young trees marking the limits of the Bayham Estate, coming out onto the main Hastings road. Then it would be downhill all the way, past an oast house, to the War Memorial and the cottage. I would push my bicycle through the narrow entrance between the two enveloping growths of tall hedge, leaving it against the side of the house. Mrs Willett would say that Wilfred was waiting for me 'in there'. Very occasionally, 'in there' would not be the wonderfully chaotic study, but the summer house at the bottom of the garden.

The first reward for the long ride would be Wilfred's absolutely wonderful smile, one of the warmest, most infectious I have ever seen. Generally he would be dressed in an old sports' coat with leather patches at the elbows and a pair of corduroy trousers. The clothes went well with the joyful disorder of the room: books and papers strewn over every flat surface, some of them half-toppled, others already spilling over into jumbled heaps. 'Chuck them off the chair', he would say, with little respect for its temporary occupants. There were even books and papers on the big fire-guard seat, which was also one of his favourite perches. I loved that untidy, well-lived-in room: in winter full of wood smoke from the damply burning, semi-choking fire; in summer, the windows onto the garden wide open, the room still vaguely smelling of smoke.

In due course, Mrs Willett would come in with tea on an enormous tray which she would prop up perilously on a leather pouf. And *what* a tea, *what* a reward for the cyclist! Quite one of the best, even by the demanding standards of Tunbridge Wells, the Tea Capital of the South of England in the 30s and 40s.

Wilfred would want to know what I had been doing since I had last seen him. He was a very good listener; but this was not just his natural politeness; he really *wanted* to know. I used to feel flattered by his obvious interest, and I think it must have been the same with all his visitors. Sometimes I would meet one on the way out of the study and would note the happiness on his or her face.

During the War years, he took a great, almost child-like, delight in the sweeping Soviet victories on the Eastern Front, victories that had amply vindicated his own beliefs. Had he not always expressed his confidence in the Red army? And this was a delight I fully shared. His enthusiasm and the sheer simplicity of his faith seemed to communicate even to Stalin something of Wilfred's own goodness, though I doubt whether Stalin were ever aware either of the strength of the devotion to him of this rather eccentric English admirer or whether he would even have been able to recognise sheer goodness when confronted with something so unusual.

It did not seem to matter, for that was not the point: it was the shining integrity of Wilfred's belief that most came through. I always came away from these conversations feeling refreshed, full of enthusiasm, *gonflé à bloc* and ready for the stiff uphill climb to the main Hastings road. Wilfred *radiated* goodness, confidence and simple joy, and I think all his visitors must have come away similarly warmed.

He was one of the best people I have ever met; and he also had a wonderful gift of making me feel important, that what I did or thought mattered and would make a difference. After all these years, I still miss him as much as ever, just as I can still see him, with his beautiful, slightly lop-sided smile, his rather bulbous and kindly eyes smiling too, hear his patient, halting speech and welcoming voice, and marvel at his ability to cope with his physical disadvantages. There he is, in his chair, surrounded by mountains of paper, or upsetting layer upon layer of books in search of some pamphlet he wanted to show me, or sitting on the fire-guard, his back to the sputtering wood fire.

He is still absolutely alive for me. He is one of those rare people who, just by being there, by being himself, has enriched my life and filled me with optimism about human nature. No wonder I would tackle the uphill return journey with such vigour, standing up on the pedals and calling out to the high hedges or to the occasional startled pedestrian! Once I had got home, my mother would not have to ask what sort of time I had had with Wilfred; she could see it in my face. She was very fond of him too.

*   *   *

In the last few months, my picture of Wilfred has been filled out, so as to include the far distant young man at the other side of the great divide of 1914 and to place him firmly among his own generation of men and girls in their early twenties by 1910 or so. This extra dimension has been provided by the photograph albums that Marjorie has shown me, dating from the greatest photographic age and one in which the family album passes down to us the many, open, utterly *trusting* faces of young men and young women: the Age of Innocence.

How Wilfred threw himself into every imaginable activity: sporting, social, military, scholastic! He seems to be constantly changing clothes: here he is in blazer and whites, in shooting dress, in shorts, in a hacking jacket, in tails and white tie, and, again and again, in uniform. I had had no inkling of this. From about 1911, till it all happened in 1914, he seems to have been consciously preparing for what was to come. Perhaps he hoped it would. He came of a generation of simple, unquestioning and utterly confident patriots, young men of his age group, similarly engaged, in England, in France, in Germany, in Italy, maybe in Russia.

It is still Wilfred; but the pre-war face is not quite the same: no sign of suffering, even a hint of arrogance, more than a hint of perfect class confidence, the face of an upper-class young Trinity man who expected much of life, knew what was due to him, had excellent prospects, a shining career stretching out ahead of him:

xviii

a houseman, perhaps a consultant, and who had demanding standards of comfort, gastronomy, and propriety. It is *almost* the face of a complete stranger; the eyes are much the same, but they are seldom smiling; and the discrepancy between the bold, rather insensitive figure of pre-1914 and the maimed Wilfred whom I had always known and greatly loved, seems almost as tragic as the framed photographs of all those elegant young officers, smooth-faced and proud of their Sam-Brownes and their swagger-sticks, in the Smoke Room of All Souls.

Almost, but not *quite* as tragic, for Wilfred lived on, learning to cope with quite a different life.

RICHARD COBB

Chairman of the 1984 Booker Prize judges.
    Author of *Still Life: Sketches of a Tunbridge Wells Childhood* (Chatto & Windus, The Bodley Head), 1983, paperback 1985.
    Professor of Modern History, University of Oxford, 1973-1984.
    The reference to Paris is to the years 1946 to 1955 when he was working on histories of revolutionary France. The reference to Aberystwyth is to the years 1955 to 1961 when he was Lecturer in History at the University College of Wales.

The Beginnings in War

1 – ORIGINS

May, 1913 – Wilfred and Eileen – young love – family origins.

For my mother an infatuation, a possessive love that was to last a lifetime, began in May 1913 in Cambridge. For my father at that time began a romantic love, a passionate involvement that might not have lasted many years had it not become so intertwined with gratitude, admiration and dependence that a stronger love for her emerged to survive the spiritual journeys he was to make from which she stood aside.

In 1913 he was a medical student at Trinity College, Cambridge. His family, the Willetts, were middle-class. His father, Thomas, was neither brilliant nor energetic, being content to amble through the law exams which made him a solicitor and thereafter to live on a comfortable income bequeathed by his father, a builder. But the genes that passed Thomas by came to his eldest son, Wilfred. They were the qualities of Huguenot forebears who arrived in Colchester, penniless for the sake of a religion proscribed in France. Descendants became pilots on the Thames, and in the 19th century builders of note in Brighton and Hove, progenitors of the firm of William Willett of Sloane Square. Wilfred's uncle, William Willett the younger, born in 1856, succeeded his father in the family building business, but the passion of his life became the campaign for daylight savings or Summer Time. Between 1907 and 1914, he wrote and distributed 15 pamphlets urging legislation to move the clocks forward in summer so that people would spend an extra hour of their waking life in daylight. He lived in a large house on Chislehurst Common and said he first thought of the idea when riding in the woods early one summer morning.

There was considerable opposition to the 'fantastic' idea of 'moving time' which, it was said, would cause chaos on the railways, in the shops and offices and on farms – the milk yield would fall if cows were milked an hour earlier. Undaunted, he bombarded Members of Parliament and well-known people with his pamphlet 'The Waste of Daylight' which went into 19 editions.

The money to support this expensive campaign was forthcoming from his business activities. He built houses for the prosperous middle-class in Brighton, Chislehurst and London. He largely inspired the design of the Sloane Square area: streets of handsome houses, with fine brickwork. He used Portland stone and tiles instead of the customary stucco.

As Wilfred grew up, William Willett and his daylight savings became a much discussed issue, almost as hotly debated as votes for women. Its opponents declared they would not be 'made into early risers by Act of Parliament'. Some of his supporters were men then or later famous in public life: Lloyd George, the First World War Prime Minster; Winston Churchill, the Second World War Prime Minster; Herbert Samuel, the Liberal leader in the 1930's; A. J. Balfour, Prime Minster from 1902 to 1906 and author of the Balfour Declaration; Austin Chamberlain, later Chancellor of the Exchequer; Keir Hardie, a founder of the Labour Party; T. P. O'Connor, for long 'father' of the House of Commons. In 1911 there was a meeting at the Guildhall at which the principal speaker was Mr Winston Churchill. He concluded with the prophecy that some day a grateful nation would erect a statue to William Willett and lay sunflowers at his feet on the longest day. Sufficient support for daylight savings had been organised by 1908 to allow Mr (later Sir) Robert Pearse to introduce a Bill into Parliament. The Bill had a second reading and was sent to a Select Committee. Despite a favourable report from the Committee, the Bill did not get a third reading because scientific opinion was divided. Sir David Gill, Astonomer Royal, complained that Sir Robert Ball, the astonomer at Cambridge, had been 'bamboozled' by Mr Willettt, who was 'so very persistent'.

The persistent Mr Willett again, in 1909, persuaded Mr Pearse

2

to re-introduce the Bill. This time it failed because the new Select Committee said '1. There is great diversity of opinion, and, 2. [There are] doubts as to whether the objects of the Bill can be obtained without giving rise to serious inconvenience to important interests.'

Wilfred was a welcome guest at Chislehurst. He and his Uncle Will liked each other, and both enjoyed early morning riding in the surrounding woods. (Their mutual affection was lasting; Wilfred always kept a letter his uncle sent to him in the trenches advising him to keep walnuts in his pockets as an iron ration. The letter was from The Cedars, Chislehurst.) It was not unusual for the chauffeur-driven car to be summoned so that Wilfred could be taken to inspect some of the firm's building work. Uncle Will sat at the back of the car with a home-made compass on his knee, directing the chauffeur through a speaking tube.

They could often be seen backing out of cul-de-sacs with the chauffeur blowing his horn and Uncle Will standing on the back seat to make sure no-one was run over.

Uncle Will's restless, inventive mind was evidently not completely satisfied with his successful business, although he never allowed his reforming missionary activities to interfere with the attention he gave it. In 1914 he invented the Willett Petrol-Air-Gas light generator intended for use in country houses in place of candles and oil lamps — 'which', as the promotional literature stated, 'may be romantic but are not economical'. Several prototypes of this machine were made, and one was in use from 1922 to after the War in 1946 in the Methodist Chapel in the Lincolnshire village of Ludford Magna.

He also invented a prototype of a telephone system that would relay live concerts into private homes on a pay-as-you-listen basis. But there is no record that this early idea of a kind of cable broadcasting was ever marketed.

Sadly, William Willett died a year before he could see the Daylight Savings Act of 1916 enacted to save precious fuel wasted on artificial light in factories and offices during the First World War. His early death, it was said at the time, had prevented recognition by a knighthood of his work as a social reformer.

3

Wilfred's mother, Susie, must also have had formidable ancestors, for she herself had all the style of a great lady which owed nothing to her origins as the daughter of a shop-keeper in Brighton. Her marriage to Thomas Willett, not welcomed at the time by his family, was all that was needed to move her toward a life-style for which she was well suited, that of the moneyed upper middle-class.

My mother, Eileen Estelle Josephine Stenhouse was 20 in 1913. Her mother, Ethel Toulmin, came from an impoverished aristocratic family, one of whose members had emigrated to America and was responsible for the Lousiana purchase, an enormous bargain for the United States. One of the family legends was that the flags would fly all over North America should any of his descendants sail past the Statue of Liberty. My mother's sister was christened Violet Nelson: another family 'cause célèbre' was to claim descent from Horatio Nelson.

My maternal grandmother, Ethel, fell in love imprudently and married a wild, red-haired Scotsman of infinite charm and an addiction to drink. If he had been steady, it would have been a good marriage financially, for he was a Stenhouse, a member of a prosperous insurance firm that has grown into Reed Stenhouse Gibbs. But he died early, leaving her with two small daughters, Violet, aged four, and my mother, aged two.

It was not long before the young widow was wooed and won by a widower, Henry Munt, a wealthy stockbroker with two grown-up daughters. He purchased a big house, 10 Ashburn Place, in Kensington — no doubt with the idea that the joint family of four girls might be increased. Twelve servants, including a coachman and my grandmother's old nurse, Pepi, made my mother's childhood comfortable and happy. Even the arrival of four half-brothers and sisters cannot have disturbed her security, for her step-father loved her as much as his own children and sent her to a good day-school for young ladies, Sussex House in Lancaster Gate, and afterwards to a finishing school in Switzerland.

2 – THE MAY BALL

Mr Munt persuaded – Wilfred and Eileen meet – Wilfred's medical career and his idealism – the London Hospital – the hotel rendezvous – secret marriage.

It was shortly after her return home that she was invited to the May Ball at Trinity College, Cambridge by a cousin, Graham Leadham.

Her step-father was reluctant to let her go. While she was in Switzerland, the family had been distressed and outraged by the elopement of the eldest Munt daughter with the coachman. Eileen, at 20, was pretty and if she went to Cambridge would have to stay the night. The disgraceful affair of his eldest daughter was a terrible warning to Mr Munt of the perilous condition of upper-class maidenhood.

Eileen pleaded sweetly:

'It will be such fun, father. I know you want me to enjoy myself, and you promised me a new ball dress for winning the prize for English at school. I may never be asked again. Do do let me go, father: I won't talk to anybody on the train and Graham will look after me'.

'Your mother and I won't have an easy minute until your return'.

This statement Eileen knew to be untrue, for the only one of her six children Mrs Munt ever worried about was her youngest child, John. However:

'Father, supposing Tol came with me [Tol was the governess] if mother would spare her? Then we could stay in a hotel and you wouldn't worry about me; and Tol could help me dress and do my hair for me. You know it always falls down when I do it myself'.

This last plea proved irresistible. Eileen arrived at Cambridge with Tol and her new dress, prepared to have a wonderful time. She was not attracted to Graham, her cousin, but she might

5

meet, almost certainly would meet, some wonderful young man, handsome and well-born, who would fall in love with her. He would give her a large diamond ring and she would be married before Violet who was engaged to a stuffy solicitor, quite nice but so old.

Thus, as she dreamed of romance with all a young girl's fantasies, Tol helped her into her champagne-coloured lace dress with a wide satin sash of the same colour as the underskirt. It had cost a lot of money but father didn't mind because it suited her so well. She had put it on to show him.

Her satin shoes were dyed to match. Tol helped her loop her hair with satin ribbon and she was ready quite half an hour before a page boy knocked on the door to tell her that a gentleman was waiting in the foyer.

Graham said, 'You look beautiful, Eileen. All the fellows will be jealous but I want you to meet some of my friends. They'll all want a dance but you must keep some gaps in your programme for me'.

The circumstances were propitious, Eileen was ready, eager, to fall in love and be loved. She had never looked more beautiful. She was modest and intelligent. These attractions combined to single her out from the crowd of girls that May night at the Trinity Ball.

One of the first friends Graham introduced her to was Wilfred Willett, a fine athlete, a sure marksman and clever as well. He was the same height as Eileen, five foot nine, so her large brown eyes, wide apart, looked straight into his unusually large grey-blue eyes, hooded with deep lids — a family characteristic as she afterwards knew when she met Wilfred's Uncle Will. She had a graceful figure with slender hands and feet, an oval face, an unfashionably wide mouth and a lovely smile. Wilfred was be-witched. She thought him distinguished-looking; she was awed by his reputation and charmed by his masterful manner. She had never met anyone like him. He was not a good dancer but she was, and so she guided him through the steps of the foxtrot.

When the band stopped playing, Wilfred still held her round the waist. 'It's the polka next, dance it with me', he whispered.

6

Eileen glanced round. Another name was written on her programme and there was the young man advancing to claim her.

'I can't', she replied. But the band struck up and Wilfred gently drew her into the midst of the dancers:

'One, two three' — and they were whirling away to the beat of the band:

'Oh, see me dance the polka . . .' someone raised his voice and many of the dancers joined the refrain. Wilfred was much better at the polka than the other dances, for his arm was strong and his feet sure as he whirled Eileen round. It was perhaps at this moment that she knew she was in love with Wilfred. The delicious awareness of mutual attraction held them both.

'Let me get your cloak', he muttered as the music stopped. 'We can go outside and walk around for a bit to cool off'.

Wrapped in her purple velvet cloak with the white silk lining, the hood framing her face, Eileen allowed him to hold her hand as they walked together and she shyly told him of her family, of some of the events of her short and sheltered life. He spoke of his work, his enthusiasm for medicine, his hopes of joining a great London Hospital to complete his studies, his ambition to succeed and his desire to alleviate suffering — two ideals so intermingled that he hardly knew which was the stronger.

Graham was cross and agitated when they finally returned to the College:

'Eileen, I promised Tol I would take you back as soon as the Ball was over, and it finished ten minutes ago. Wilfred, it's too bad of you to keep Eileen out'.

Scarcely time to touch each other's hands, and Eileen was walking off with Graham. Wilfred heard her low but clear voice apologising as she went.

Thus began a time of such entrancing happiness that the outside world vanished to a pinpoint. Wilfred supposed he must have worked, for his exam results were outstanding. Eileen lost all sense of duty to her family as she weaved ever more skilful lies about her whereabouts. Old friends, relatives, were shamelessly used as she plotted to spend days with Wilfred at Cambridge:

'Mary Lester has asked me to lunch'.

'I thought I'd visit Aunt Flo at Richmond'.

'There's a lecture I thought I'd go to. No, it's not a suffragette meeting, I don't want to get mixed up in all that'.

Her mother was easy to deceive. Mr Munt was having a worrying time with his business interests. Violet, whose sharp eyes might have noticed Eileen's glowing face when she returned from one of these expeditions, was preoccupied with her own forthcoming marriage.

The idyllic months fled past. Wilfred was to leave Cambridge and become a medical student at the London Hospital. He thought it would be easier for them to meet when they were both in London. Eileen thought it would be more difficult. There was no privacy in the London parks. The precious afternoons picnicking on the river bank at Cambridge, the private talks, the kisses, the embraces, urgent but still restrained. All this must be given up. And Wilfred's hours at the London Hospital would be much longer, his spare time more unpredictable, his studies more demanding.

'Why can't we be engaged', she urged him at a meeting in a tea-shop near the hospital. 'My parents won't like it because they'll say you can't support me. But I can say we are prepared to be engaged until you qualify.'

'My parents will just stop my allowance,' he said, reaching for her hand under the table. 'They won't hear of it. No, we'd better go on seeing each other when we can'.

Frustration and anxiety began to affect Eileen's health. Wilfred was working so hard. Because of this he was often irritable and he expected her to understand if they managed to meet only once a week.

Mr Munt noticed her pallor and listlessness and ordered her to see the family doctor, but nothing was found to be wrong.

'Girls often are highly strung at Eileen's age,' Mrs Munt remarked comfortingly to her husband. 'It's bound to pass. When Violet is married and she is the only daughter "out", she'll start to bloom again'.

One day Eileen met Wilfred and told him she had booked a room at the Russell Hotel. 'We're never alone,' she said, 'so I went into the Reception and booked a room for the night and

8

said my brother would be visiting me and we'd have dinner together. I shan't stay the night, of course, but they think at home that I am going to a concert with a friend and will come home by cab when it's over.'

Wilfred was embarrassed by the suspicious stare of the commissionaire as they entered the lift after dinner. He was sullen and unresponsive when they were alone in the bedroom and Eileen's happy mood vanished and she burst into tears.

'You don't love me!' she sobbed.

'I do, and that's the trouble. We shall have to marry. I've been thinking about it and I'm going to get a licence. You will have to say you're 21. We can be married at Marylebone Registry Office.'

'Our parents will be shocked and your allowance will be stopped. You said so.'

'We shan't tell anyone. Only you and I will know that we belong to each other. Some day, when I'm qualified, we will announce it in *The Times* and have all our relations to a celebration party.'

Neither Wilfred nor Eileen supposed that their relations would see any cause for a celebration. Mrs Willett had met Eileen, and dislike had been mutual. The Munts had thought Wilfred a pleasant young man but:

'I understand his people are in trade, dear', Mrs Munt remarked to Eileen: 'Building, isn't it? Perhaps you shouldn't see too much of him. I thought the young man Graham brought to tea last week much nicer. He's related to the Seymours'.

Wilfred was amazed at Eileen's tranquillity as the weeks went by while he arranged the marriage. He was too busy at the hospital, too anxious to do well to worry as much as he would otherwise have done at the thought of his formidable mother finding out. However, not only had the relationship reached a stage when he knew their love for each other would soon be fully consummated, but Eileen's insistence on seeing him so often was getting in the way of his work. When they were married she would be content to see him less, he thought.

Eileen was frightened of losing him to one of the pretty nurses she had seen at the hospital. He might meet a girl who could talk interestingly about public affairs, music and art: things Wilfred knew about and she didn't. The thought of losing him troubled her sleep at night and many of her waking moments. Now they would be married. He would be hers:

'Till death us do part' she whispered to herself as they left the Registry Office.

Ringed Plovers

3 − RUMOURS OF WAR

Together at last − Wilfred's patriotism − he volunteers −
Susie Willett and the Fifth Commandent − official church
wedding − Susie stays away − Army Camp, Crowborough.

Not long after their marriage, Eileen told Wilfred she had taken a
bed-sitting room in a street near the hospital. He was astonished
at her initiative:

'However did you find it?' he said. 'Can we afford it?'

'I asked in the post office,' she replied 'and they told me that
Mrs Hicks was a widow and looking for a boarder. I went to see
her and explained we were married but couldn't see much of
each other as you would be living in the hospital most of the time
and I had to look after an invalid mother. She was very nice
about it and has put a table in the room where you can work. It's
very cheap and we can pay half each from our allowances.'
Wilfred began to realise that Eileen was a much stronger
character than he had thought.

As the year passed, Eileen bloomed with happiness. Wilfred
loved her more than ever now that they could lie together in Mrs
Hicks little bedroom. He had never imagined marriage would
be such shared joy.

Yet a worry appeared. He occasionally met some of his old
friends from Cambridge and they were excited at the thought of
a coming war with Germany. They were all joining territorial
regiments. And Wilfred himself, without telling Eileen, had
joined the London Rifle Brigade. He had been in the Officer
Training Corps at Cambridge and was quickly gazetted as 2nd
Lieutenant in the L.R.B.

Eileen was 22 on 4 August 1914, the day War broke out.
Wilfred did not want to spoil her birthday but the following day
he told her he intended to 'fight for England'.

'Fight for England? But you don't have to! You'll be qualified in a few months' time and doctors will be wanted in England. Besides, it'll all be over by Christmas!'

'That's just it,' said Wilfred. 'It will be, but I want to have done my bit for my country. You know how I feel about England,' he pleaded, trying to take her hand.

She snatched it away. Wilfred had never seen her in such a rage. The quarrel grew so loud that they heard Mrs Hicks knocking on the door:

'Whatever's the matter?' she called.

'Nothing to worry about,' said Wilfred, opening the door. By this time Eileen lay sobbing on the bed.

A few days later Eileen was calmer but still distracted with worry, refusing to believe she couldn't make him change his mind.

Wilfred said they had to tell their parents they were married. 'I shall be going into training at Crowborough in Kent,' he told her, 'and you'll be able to come with me. But your parents must know about it. Besides, there's a rumour that we shall sail for France after a few weeks of training and I don't want to leave England with no-one knowing you're my wife'.

Breaking the news to their parents was traumatic. Mrs Willett had hysterics. Mr Willett was very grave and talked about ingratitude. Eileen's parents were distressed but consoled because Wilfred would be a professional man. It all passed over Eileen's head. Her thoughts were centred absolutely on the parting with Wilfred, the possibility of danger, the fear of losing him.

Wilfred had had a very difficult evening with his parents as he told Eileen in one of the few times they now managed to meet at Mrs Hicks':

'It was awful,' he said. 'Mater went on and on about deceit and the Fifth Commandment. Finally, she felt so faint that Pater had had to help her up the stairs to bed. He came back and said that he was going to see your father today so that arrangements could be made for us to be married 'properly.'

He glanced at Eileen and an involuntary smile parted her lips. They collapsed on the bed laughing. Wilfred was relieved to see that Eileen could see the funny side of anything; her mood latterly had been so sombre, almost sullen.

A few days later the marriage was arranged by special licence in Eileen's parish church. Eileen told Wilfred that she was to have a new cream dress:

'Mother thinks white would be unsuitable, under the circumstances,' she said, glancing slyly at him.

'I agree, the circumstances are thoroughly unsuitable and I vote for continuing to make them so.'

'Also,' continued Eileen, some minutes later, 'Mother is very annoyed with your mother making such a fuss as if I weren't good enough for you, considering the noble Earl, three times removed, and Nelson and all that. But of course I told her that I'm not good enough for you because you are so clever and everyone thinks you are going to be in Wimpole Street one day'.

The marriage, as Wilfred and Eileen agreed, was a dismal affair. Mrs Willett didn't attend. 'She's far too upset,' Wilfred's father muttered as they entered the church. But Wilfred was comforted by the service. He had always been a devout Christian, and to have his marriage sanctified dissipated the fleeting guilt he had felt because they had been married in a registry office.

Eileen had had no such feelings. The vows they made to each other were the important, the most moving, part of the ceremony:

'I, Wilfred Leslie, take thee Eileen . . .'

'I, Eileen Estelle Josephine, take thee Wilfred . . .'

The tears brimmed from her eyes as he placed the ring on her finger. How much longer would they have before he went to the war? She thrust the thought aside.

Soon Wilfred was in training at Crowborough and, after a few days, he found rooms for her in a nearby cottage. Time hung heavily in the long hours she waited for him to join her, sometimes only for an hour before daybreak. She spent much time sitting before the fire with a book on her knee or restlessly walking round the little room, peering through the window to see if Wilfred was approaching. Wilfred had lent her some of his natural history books and notebooks; he had kept the notebooks since he was a boy, on holiday in Norfolk. She wanted to

13

concentrate on the reading because she knew it would please him. But her attention wandered. Sometimes it seemed as though she was listening to screams, unuttered but full of anguish:

'Wilfred, Wilfred, don't leave me. Life is you and me. How can I live if you never come back. Wilfred!'

He had wanted a photograph of her. She found one and wrote on the back: 'From your wee wifie'. She was as tall as he, but in character she couldn't match him. He put it in his pocket book.

Towards the end of October, all ranks were inoculated against typhoid. Officers' kits were to be no more than 35lbs including valise. Wilfred reluctantly discarded his warm camel hair and cashmere sleeping bag he had had since he was at St Paul's School. On 27 October Wilfred came to tell Eileen that the adjutant had received embarkation orders. The anguished parting was short but the following night, as Eileen sobbed quietly on her bed, Wilfred appeared. The order had been cancelled. He lay by her on the bed, her head on his shoulder. Neither spoke.

There were two more meetings and then mercifully, while they were still expecting to see each other again, the battalion struck camp at night. It was 3 November.

Lapwing in Flight

4 — FRANCE

Wilfred's sadness lightened and his spirits rose as the Band of the
Post Office Rifles played cheerful military music as the L.R.B.
troops marched to the station to entrain for Southampton. They
embarked on S.S. Chyebassa on the evening of 4 November
and, after a calm crossing, disembarked at Havre on the next
day. A long, exhausting march followed to No. 1 Rest Camp,
already occupied by troops who had been in the front line. The
L.R.B. men had to spend a frosty night in the open as there were
not enough tents. Rations were short, the bully beef
unaccountably lost. Wilfred went among his men trying to cheer
them up. Physical discomfort had made them depressed, a
receptive audience for the alarming stories told by the seasoned
troops. Wilfred had already become popular during the training
at Crowborough and now the men looked up to him and
believed everything he said.

The following day 848 men, 22 vehicles, 2 machine guns and
68 horses were accommodated with difficulty in a train of 50
trucks. They reached St Omer on 7 November and marched 3½
miles to the Cavalry barracks at Wisques. Disappointment was
keen. The barracks, a disused convent, was dirty. No water, no
fireplaces, no means of lighting. Wilfred cheered his men, as did
the other officers, and after a day or two some of the
shortcomings were remedied.

During the First Battle of Ypres, the L.R.B. with one or two
other territorial battalions and the North Somerset Infantry were
the only troops in reserve in the whole British Expeditionary
Force, and had to be ready to move at any time. The short

respite at the cavalry barracks enabled the men to practise rapid loading, but the rifles converted to take the new service ammunition were not entirely satisfactory. Someone had blundered.

Wilfred's fondness for animals was well known, and he was depressed when one of the big transport horses, the Pride of Hammersmith, collapsed and died. Burying him was a difficult and lengthy task; the ground was very hard.

Altogether it was a tense and trying time. Even for an officer, the conditions which had to be endured were worse than he had ever experienced. But his letters to Eileen continued to tell her that he was well and cheerful, and in no danger.

She read these letters over and over again in her bedroom at Ashburn Place. She tried to make an effort when the family met for meals but it was a pitiful failure. Often she got up hastily and left before she was seized with another bout of weeping.

'Eileen is like a lost soul', said Mrs Munt crossly. 'Goodness knows, if everyone who had a husband or son in France behaved like her, I declare that everything would stop running.'

'Early days, early days,' Mr Munt replied. 'Eileen will settle down in a week or two for sure.'

Meanwhile Wilfred with the L.R.B. had arrived at Romarin, close to the heavy fighting which had taken place since October at Ploegsteert. It was 19 November.

The 1st Somerset Light Infantry had been holding a line from the River Douve to Le Gleer village but on 1 November they had been driven back by heavy artillery fire. On 7 November the Inniskillings made a gallant attempt to drive the Germans out of Ploegsteert Wood and lost 5 officers and 50 men in the vain attack.

The arrival of the London Rifle Brigade on 22 November to take up billets in the village were the much wanted reinforcements.

Two days before, on 20 November, the first casualty was sustained by the battalion. Rifleman J. Dunnett, only 18, was killed by a stray shell while having breakfast. Wilfred thought that the universal shock and sadness of this death, which he felt himself, was the reaction of civilians. The men had not yet been in battle, had not yet become inured to death as they would have to become in a very short while.

Working Parties were soon set up to convert Bunhill Row, half a mile behind the front line, into a line of defence and to lay down paths through the mud which had made the ground all round the woods and village almost impassable.

The soil was clay. Big lumps fell off the side of the trenches which were two feet deep in icy water. Everyone's boots and puttees became soaking wet. Wilfred and the other officers struggled to keep themselves clean as befitted their rank. Few of the officers and none of the men had been able to have a bath since leaving England, almost a month earlier.

These insanitary conditions were remedied early in December when a brewery on the road to Armentières, a hundred yards south of where the L.R.B. Cemetry now lies, was converted into a bath house. Boilers were mended to heat the water and big brewing vessels became baths.

The fighting between the Germans holding Ploegsteert Wood and battalions of the Somerset and Essex Regiments and the L.R.B. intensified. In the second week in December, the edge of the wood was recaptured and also some of the houses used by snipers.

On 13 December, Wilfred was supervising some shoring-up work in one of the trenches when one of the men called that Sergeant Moore had been hit while outside the trenches and was lying, wounded, some yards from the L.R.B. lines.

Wilfred snatched up the special medical kit he always kept near him and climbed out of the trench. He saw the wounded man still conscious, some yards away, and knelt down to examine his shattered leg. He thought he would dress and bandage the wound before he called out the stretcher bearers. Instead he fell foward in the mud, hit in the head by a sniper's bullet.

Perfectly conscious, Wilfred looked up into the shocked faces of the men who were lifting him onto the stretcher. He thought he must look a mess, for he could feel the warm blood on his face. Probably hit in the Broca and Rolandic areas of his skull, he thought, his medical knowledge automatically alerted. He tried

17

to speak to tell the men how to lift the wounded sergeant. No words came.

Periods of consciousness and unconsciousness, sickness and pain, and, finally, a coma filled the intervening days before he arrived at the Base Hospital at Boulogne. He thought he asked for Eileen but the nurse turned away as if she hadn't heard. Sometimes his thoughts were coherent and fretful because, surely, he should be X-rayed or operated on? Once he opened his eyes and saw a doctor, at least he thought it was a doctor. But he felt confused and ill and closed his eyes again.

In London, Eileen was worried because his last letter was dated 10 December. Now it was the 19th. She made her way to the L.R.B. Headquarters and asked to see the duty officer. She explained her anxiety. He sympathised, but told her there was no news.

On 20 December she heard that Wilfred was 'gravely wounded' and at the Base Hospital in Boulogne.

Eileen now had one thought only: how could she reach Wilfred? She asked her father. He told her it was unlikely that she would, as a civilian, be able to get a passport to travel to France. Eileen went to the War Office, and then to the Foreign Office. Here she was at first refused. Finally, either to remove her haunting presence, or in response to her tragic face and tearful pleas, she was given a document signed by Sir Edward Grey, the Foreign Secretary, entitling the bearer, Mrs Eileen Estelle Josephine Willett, aged 22, to travel to France. It was dated 22 December 1914.

She arrived at the hospital, was shown to the ward where Wilfred lay, white and still, most of his head hidden under bandages. His hands lay outside the covers. She knelt by the bed and clasped them, laid her face against his cheek while her tears fell onto his bandages.

The doctors, she found, did not want Wilfred moved to England. They told her, quite bluntly, that they did not think he would live. Very little was known about the treatment of head wounds. They had not been a major cause of casualty in previous wars. Steel helmets were not issued until 1916. In that year an American specialist in brain surgery revolutionised the

18

treatment of head injuries. But now it was 1914, and many with severe head wounds died or were paralysed who would have been saved later in the War.

Every day Eileen waited outside the office of the R.A.M.C. officer in charge of the hospital. Every day she requested that arrangements be made to return her husband to England. So many other casualties were coming in that the hospital was hard pressed to accommodate them all. Wilfred's bed could be used for another wounded officer. The Commanding Officer, after resistance and warnings, signed the order. Wilfred's return to England was under way.

Eileen had felt that Wilfred might die if he were not moved. In the few days she had watched by his bedside, she had seen no signs of improvement. Sometimes he seemed to know her and she thought she felt a slight pressure from his left hand on hers. But he still could not speak and his periods of consciousness seemed to be lessening. She slept very little but, once she knew they would be returning to England, her spirits lifted.

'Now he will not die,' she told one of the nurses who had been very kind to her. 'I know that once we are in England, he will get better.'

The nurse pressed her hand and turned away. She was glad she would not see Eileen's grief when he died.

5 – ENGLAND

Belgrave Square – Dr Dawson – the Duchess of Norfolk –
London Hospital – surgery – 'autogene' – saved but
paralysed – career in medicine lost – a life in writing?

Wilfred seemed to bear the journey well. He was no worse when
he was finally put to bed in the Duchess of Norfolk's home for
convalescent officers in Belgrave Square.

Eileen remained hopeful for a few weeks. Wilfred could say a
few words but could not manage sentences. He was pleased to
have visits from Eileen's parents and his own, but tired quickly.
Then one day when Eileen was sitting by his bedside he had a
convulsion.

The following day Eileen went to see Dr Dawson (later Lord
Dawson of Penn). Wilfred had been in his 'team' at the London
Hospital. Eileen had had a letter from him saying how sad he
was that so 'brilliant a student' should have been so severely
wounded in the performance of a gallant deed.

Eileen described Wilfred's condition to Dr Dawson. He asked
her if Wilfred had been X-rayed or operated on.

'No, he has not,' replied Eileen.

'Then from what you tell me he almost certainly has splinters
of bone in his brain. They must be causing pressure. There may
be an abscess.

'If we had him here, we could deal with that. One of my
colleagues is interested in brain surgery and he would tell us if it
is possible to remove the fragments which are preventing your
husband's recovery.'

'Dr Dawson, please find room for Wilfred in this hospital. I
am so frightened about him.' Her voice dropped and her eyes
beseeched him.

'Difficult. He's under the Army's care, you see. However, if
you will arrange to get him out of Belgrave Square and bring him
here, a bed will be found for him. That, I promise.'

He looked at her as she nodded her head and then, speaking as if reluctantly, said:

'Of course I haven't seen him yet, but I think you must know before making the decision to move him that, although we may save his life, he is certain to be left with physical damage because he had not been operated on earlier. He will be paralysed in some degree, his speech may be impaired. And another possibility, more remote, is that he may not be able to give you children. Have you thought of that?'

'We've talked about children, of course, but I always thought Wilfred wanted a family more than I did. I would like Wilfred's children. I don't want anyone else's. And about the paralysis, I've thought about that too and, Dr Dawson, I would sooner live with Wilfred paralysed than live without him'.

'Then you've made the decision for yourself. But you see he is not able to say what he wants. He will die if he stays where he is. Indeed, he may die if he comes here. But would he want to live, handicapped as he will be, giving up medicine, as he must?'

'I don't know what he would want but I know that I can't let him die. May I bring him here tomorrow?'

'An amazing young woman,' thought Dr Dawson, as he held the door for her. 'We shall have to save her husband's life if we can.'

Eileen decided to ask for her step-father's help about transporting Wilfred. The Willetts would try to prevent it. Mrs Willett had convinced herself that it was only a matter of time before Wilfred recovered and, meanwhile, he had the personal interest of 'the dear Duchess of Norfolk'. The Duchess had made a special point of congratulating Mr and Mrs Willett on their son's Mention in Dispatches, signed by Winston S. Churchill, Secretary of State for War, 'for gallant and distinguished conduct in the field'. No, Eileen decided, they mustn't know about it until he is in the London Hospital.

Mr Munt's real love for Eileen showed as he kissed her tenderly when she made her request. He told her that he would arrange and pay for a private ambulance to come to Belgrave Square. Eileen must watch for its arrival and take the attendants with their stretcher to Wilfred's bedside. It would have to be done in this secret way, he explained, because Wilfred was still in the Army: permission to have him moved would have to come from the military superintendent, a doctor whom Eileen had found unhelpful when she had talked to him about Wilfred's condition.

Eileen told Wilfred that he was to be moved to the London Hospital. He understood and said a word that might have been 'good'. His mind and his thoughts were much less confused and he knew the meaning of the convulsion he had experienced.

The removal was not as uneventful as Eileen had hoped. The ambulance attendants lifted Wilfred onto the stretcher and, with Eileen following, had reached the hall when the Duchess appeared, having been summoned by the sister-in-charge.

'Mrs Willett, what are you doing with that patient?' demanded the Duchess. 'I order those men to take him straight back to the ward or I won't answer for the consequences.'

Eileen rounded on the Duchess, fear and determination in her voice:

'My husband is leaving whether you allow it or not. Please stand aside and let the men take him to the ambulance.'

'How dare you, you wicked girl. You're going to kill him. You'll kill him, I say!'

Eileen was trembling as she finally got into the ambulance with Wilfred, the Duchess's words ringing in her ears. She had been strong and determined, but supposing the Duchess was right?

Wilfred was operated on within the following days. The skilful surgeon, in a long operation, removed all the bone fragments which had been irritating his brain. But his condition remained critical. Eileen did not leave the hospital. The sympathetic nurses and medical staff tolerated her constant presence. When the doctors visited him, she looked at them with imploring eyes and waited outside the room. The surgeon spoke to her again on the third day:

'He is holding his own,' he said, 'but I had hoped for a few more signs of general improvement. I believe it will come'.

However, on the following day Wilfred had another terrifying convulsion. Dr Dawson told Eileen they feared another abscess had formed.

'We shall drain it,' he said, 'but it's not good news.'

Wilfred tried to speak to Eileen as she sat by his bed. She told the house surgeon when he came in that she thought Wilfred was trying to say a word that sounded like 'autogene'. 'He means "autogenous vaccine",' said the young man. 'I'll tell Dr Dawson.'

Whether or not Wilfred saved his own life with this suggestion, as Eileen always believed, the vaccine was given and a rapid improvement began. Dr Dawson told Eileen they were now sure of Wilfred's life, but it would be weeks before they could say how much paralysis would be permanent. They thought he would soon be able to speak quite coherently although some impairment would probably remain.

Eileen was content. She sat by Wilfred's bed and held his hand. He could smile at her now. She considered the future and hoped she could make it happy for him. They were young and would be together.

Wilfred was in the London Hospital for many weeks. There followed a period at a convalescent home in the country. Eileen stayed nearby and her bright face helped him through times of depression and frustration when the joy of being alive — he had expected to die, he told Eileen — gave way to the bitterness of knowing that he would never be able to run again, never be able to use his right arm and hand. The paralysis of his right side was permanent.

Eileen thought his spirits would be better if they found a home together. Both sets of parents agreed and a cottage was rented for them in Sussex. Here Wilfred decided to make use of the life that Eileen had saved. He taught himself to write with his left hand and found he could walk quite fast with a stick. His physical strength enabled him to do many things that others with similar disabilities would not have attempted.

Eileen was happy that living in the country had rekindled his interest in nature. He lay in his bed or leaned back in his armchair watching the birds pecking at a lump of suet which Eileen had tied to a long piece of string and hung on the branch of a tree near the windows of the cottage. He had been an enthusiastic member of the natural history society at St Paul's School. A master, C. J. Cornish, a well known writer on natural history at the beginning of the century, had encouraged him to study bird life and write down his own observations. Natural history became an abiding hobby.

One day he said to Eileen:

'I think we should buy our own place. I'd like somewhere with a garden and woods nearby. I sometimes used to feel that, if I hadn't wanted to be a doctor, I'd have wanted to write. Perhaps I might try when we're in our own home'.

Blackbird in Nest

24

PART II

The Peaceful Years

1 – THE ROSERY

Susie Willett – jealousy – whose home? a tiff – learning to write – the ash tray – reconciliation.

The Rosery was a small Georgian house in the village of Matfield, three miles from Paddock Wood and five miles from Tunbridge Wells.

Wilfred's mother had suggested the area because she and Mr Willett had recently purchased a large Edwardian house, The Homestead, in Tunbridge Wells. She knew that Wilfred wouldn't want to live in a town so she had made several expeditions in her chauffeur-driven car – a recent acquisition – to nearby villages. She heard that a pretty old house with a large garden had been put up for sale by a Miss Reeves, a middle-aged spinster, who owned and managed one of the three 'general stores and provisions' shops in Matfield. She inspected the property and wrote to Wilfred to say she would drive down to Sussex to see them, take them to lunch at a hotel, and then to see The Rosery, Matfield.

Wilfred and Eileen liked the house and the village. The small rooms with low ceilings were very different from the London home in which Eileen had grown up, but she thought they were cosy; and the peaceful surroundings, the big trees and thick hedges where birds would nest, were exactly right for Wilfred's rehabilitation. Her dislike for Mrs Willett, which she still had, was tempered by gratitude for the trouble she had taken to find such a perfect home for them. Mrs Willett was still not fond of Eileen. Her possessive love for Wilfred would not allow her to suppress the jealousy she felt, and would have felt no matter whom he had married. Wilfred's cousin, Dolly, had recently said that it was lucky that Wilfred had married before he was wounded because his disability would have made it difficult for him to find a wife. But Dolly was put down sharply by her aunt, who told her Wilfred still had a mother who would have been quite capable of looking after him. She personally thought it was a pity Wilfred's pension would now be strained to provide for a wife as well as himself. Furthermore, she and Mr Willett would have to provide an allowance to enable Wilfred to run a separate home.

The Rosery was not furnished. Mrs Willett pointed out it would need redecorating throughout. However, the price of £400 was not excessive and Wilfred's parents and Eileen's would buy it for them.

Wilfred managed to find suitable words to express his gratitude for this generosity. Eileen's were more perfunctory. Her step-father had always been kind to her and she was unwilling to show much appreciation to Wilfred's mother for a gesture she felt he had earned from his parents. She was not free of jealousy herself, for she held the paradoxical view that she wanted Wilfred to have all that would make him happy, yet at the same time she wanted to be the one who gave it to him.

Eileen was never, throughout her life, interested in furnishing or home decoration. No change of furniture had ever been made at Ashburn Place, and when a room was redecorated the colours and style were not changed. Thus she agreed readily to her mother-in-law's suggestion that she supervise the furnishing, painting and wallpapering of The Rosery. They were in the car, returning to Sussex, when the proposition was made and Eileen's mind was on Wilfred. The day had been tiring for him. He looked pale. She hoped that her mother-in-law would not linger when they arrived home for she wanted to settle Wilfred in an armchair, with his feet up, and bring him the tea and bread and butter he always enjoyed.

Wilfred's mind was pleasurably occupied in thinking about his new home. He had already sorted out his nature notebooks and attempted to start a new one but he still needed practice in writing with his left hand. Eileen was helping him by taking down dictated notes, but he was optimistic he would soon be more proficient. His general condition had improved, although he still had difficulty with reading and transposed words both in

Mrs Seager, Wilfred's maternal grandmother, about 1860. 'Wilfred's mother, Susie, must have had formidable ancestors . . .' (p. 4).

Left to right: Thomas, Kate, Wilfred, Lewis (seated), Tintagel, 1911. 'Wilfred's father [Thomas], who qualified as a solicitor and retired at 28, . . .' (p. 29).

Left to right: Lewis, friend, Wilfred, Susie, Cousin Dolly who '. . . had sold suffragette newspapers outside South Kensington Station.' (p. 179), Tintagel, 1911.

William Willett, the younger. 'The passion of his life became the campaign for daylight savings or Summer Time' (p. 1).

THE DAYLIGHT SAVING BILL

and September. It would be specially appreciated by those who take their holidays in the latter months, as their enjoyment would not be curtailed by darkness setting in so soon after tea.

5. The effect of the scheme would be to make the day fit man's requirements more closely. We should simply replace a working day containing a certain number of hours of sunlight, by another containing one hour of sunlight more—and that in the only period now available, to most people, for leisure and recreation.

6. The following diagrams illustrate how this will operate.

AT PRESENT.

IN FUTURE IF THE BILL BE PASSED.

Each diagram represents 24 hours in June, from 7 a.m. to 7 a.m., in the case of a person rising at 7 a.m., working from 8 a.m. to 6 p.m., and going to bed at 11 p.m. The white spaces represent daylight, the dark spaces, darkness.

A page from a Willett pamphlet on the Daylight Saving Bill, 1908.

'In 1914 he invented the Willett Petrol-Air-Light Generator' (p. 3).

Top right: Wilfred at Cambridge in 1910.

Top left: Pollock caught at Tintagel in 1911. Wilfred with Kate, the Norfolk rector's daughter he '. . . loved passionately when they were both 18' (p. 105).

Left to right: S. B. Rudkin, Wilfred, B. D. Armstrong. Last day of Easter Term, St Paul's School, 1908.

*The Trinity College Rifle Club team which 'won the celebrated Wale Plate in 1911'
(p. 126). Left to right: E. L. Frost, C. F. Howard, W. L. Willett, captain (seated),
J. S. Harrowing.*

The Trinity Rugger Boat 1911 (Wilfred seated on bank).

e voices and the laughter of his friends,
happy days' (p. 132).

Wilfred, front row; Susie, second row behind and to right of Wilfred. Military Tournament, Cambridge University, Officers' Training Corps, 1911.

May Week, Cambridge, 1911.

Comrades in arms, Cambridge OTC, 1910. Left to right: Renwick, Raikes, Mewman, Mackenzie, Rosam, Willett, Romanis.

Captain Thornton, Rifle Brigade, Cambridge Degree Day, 1911.

Wilfred as sportsman with his springer spaniel, Floss, Wisborough Green, 1912.

Cambridge OTC at Training Camp, Isle of Wight, 1912. '. . . old friends from Cambridge . . . were excited at the thought of a coming war with Germany. They were all joining territorial regiments . . . Wilfred . . . was quickly gazetted a 2nd Lieutenant in the L.R.B.' (p. 11).

The War of 1914-1918.

London Regiment (T.F.)

2nd Lt. W. L. Willett

was mentioned in a Despatch from

Field Marshal Sir John D. P. French, G.C.B., O.M., G.C.V.O., K.C.M.G.

dated 14th January 1915.

for gallant and distinguished services in the Field.

I have it in command from the King to record His Majesty's

high appreciation of the services rendered.

Winston S. Churchill

War Office
Whitehall. S.W.
1st March 1919.

Secretary of State for War.

Eileen

speaking and writing. He thought The Rosery a jolly little place and imagined how the drawing room would look with his books against the walls. The room was narrow but long, having been converted from two smaller rooms. The main fireplace, lined with blue tiles with a mantelpiece above it, was in the front part of the room. The small fireplace at the other end could be covered up and a desk for himself put in front of it.

He put this idea eagerly to his mother.

She smiled indulgently. 'You can be sure I shall arrange everything for your comfort, dear,' she replied.

Although this was exactly what Eileen wanted, she couldn't repress some irritation that no mention was made of *her* comfort.

As Mrs Willett left them, she promised to get everything ready for them quickly as soon as the sale was completed.

In March 1916, Wilfred and Eileen stepped out of the hired car at the gate of The Rosery. Eileen carried her pekinese, Chou, through the white gate lying between the two huge yew bushes, and up the little path to the front door. Thick stems of virginia creeper ran up the walls and over the top of the porch, picturesque with its pitched tiled roof. The house had been aptly named; in summer the front was covered in a mass of tiny white roses.

Mrs Willett opened the door herself, a maid in white cap and apron hovering behind her. She said her chauffeur would soon arrive to drive her back to Tunbridge Wells but, meanwhile, she would await their verdict on 'her labours', she said, smiling.

Wilfred and Eileen were astonished by the thick carpets, the brass and china ornaments, the polished mahogany furniture in the drawing room, the old oak in the dining room. Every room had been furnished down to the last detail and white paint gleamed everywhere.

Although Wilfred was dismayed when his mother told him he owed her half his war gratuity for the furnishings and decorations, he was delighted with everything and told Eileen so when, at last, they were alone and sitting on the sofa before the glowing drawing room fire. To his surprise, Eileen replied tartly:

'If we'd done it ourselves, we might not have done it so grandly, but it would have been our home and not a replica of

27

your parents'. I think she might have asked us before she sold those two chairs we bought. And she has had shelves put up instead of using your bookcases, which aren't anywhere'.

'But it *is* our home. And I think you're very ungrateful. Why, Mater told us she'd unpacked my books herself and put them on the shelves.'

'That's just because she wants you to admire her. You don't seem to mind that she shows all the time she wishes you hadn't married me!.'

Wilfred had always had a quick temper, inherited, no doubt, from his grandfather, the founder of the family business. William Willett, the elder, was once said to have thrown a gravy tureen at the parlour maid.

Wilfred had managed to control his temper in earlier years but the head wound had diminished his ability to do this and now, furious with Eileen for not admiring his mother's work, he picked up an ash tray from the small mahogany table and threw it at her. It was a feeble throw, with his left hand, and she sprang to her feet so it missed her. However the erratic movement sent the dainty table spinning and the oil lamp fell to the floor. Fortunately it went out.

Eileen screamed. The dog began to bark shrilly.

'Whatever has happened, sir?' said Clara, the new maid, who came rushing in.

'Bring a light. I just knocked the lamp over as I got up to get a book,' lied my father, in fear of being suspected of bad behaviour towards his wife, of which he was now ashamed. Eileen had run upstairs and locked herself in the bathroom.

The lamp re-lit and the maid back in the kitchen cooking the dinner, Wilfred talked softly through the locked door, apologising for his violence and urging Eileen to come out and make it up. She did so almost immediately, crying as she hugged him.

28

2 – MATFIELD PEOPLE

Tennis – bridge – 'the top drawer' – Mrs Henry Storr – 'the grenadier' – Mrs Minshull – the confectioners – Zippor Buggs – the Castles – Miss Childs – Major Hoare – Siegfried Sassoon's village cricket – Mr Owles' laundry – Mr Chacksfield the butcher – Miss Reeves – the Misses Beech.

Despite the incident of the violent quarrel, no doubt relished in the village in a more or less correct version (Clara was 'walking out' with Algernon Dodd, a member of a village family), Wilfred and Eileen soon become popular members of the 'gentry'. Their story was known, the War was still on, gallantry was never more admired, and the retired soldiers and spinster ladies of Matfield were ready to attribute any unorthodox behaviour to the war wound.

Most of the people in the dozen large houses in Matfield were retired, or had enough money to live on without working. Some of the retired people had worked a little longer than Wilfred's father, who qualified as a solicitor and retired at 28, but clearly it was a pleasant life to be idle in Matfield on a comfortable income. Wilfred, whose disposition was different, gradually began to work in his garden and, with Eileen's help, to record his bird observations. Before long he was able to arrange some of the material in the form of letters and short articles in the local newspaper. The following year, to the tremendous gratification of his mother, a piece appeared in *The Times*.

The ladies in the village mostly were heavily involved in church affairs, giving the vicar no peace. And in the Women's Institute and the Mothers' Union the gentry and the villagers met on a more or less equal footing. Tennis parties and bridge parties, frequently held at The Rosery, as well as other houses, were limited to 'the top drawer', a phrase Eileen's mother often used but Wilfred disliked.

29

Eileen was asked to join various church and parish activities but refused. Her inclination was against such communal affairs, but her excuse that she couldn't leave Wilfred on his own was readily accepted.

Their first 'caller' was Mrs Storr, the widow of a vicar of Matfield. She was an intimidating visitor for an inexperienced young woman. Clara's unusually obsequious manner as she showed Mrs Storr in warned Eileen that she was about to meet someone with powerful influence in the village. Wilfred was having the afternoon rest which the doctors had ordered at this stage in his recovery.

Mrs Storr advanced towards Eileen and then paused, her gaze sweeping a table on which lay a pack of playing cards.

'Those, my dear, are the devil's playthings,' she said, both manner and voice censorious. 'I beg you to put them out of the house.'

Eileen wilted at the commanding tone but bravely invited her visitor to take a seat and rang the bell for Clara to bring tea.

As Eileen reported to Wilfred later, an interrogation followed. Eileen was asked whether she would be a regular communicant at the church and whether she would be attending both morning and evening services — 'as I always advise young married people,' Mrs Storr said.

Then, with an abrupt switch of subject, she said she would like to warn Eileen that she was paying Clara and Hetty Dodd, sister of Clara's 'intended', the other maid, more than was usual in the village. ('How did she know?' wondered Eileen.)

'High wages make for discontent and set a bad example,' Mrs Storr continued.

The lecture on domestic servants marked the end of the visit, much to Eileen's relief. She subsequently discovered, from Clara, that the Storrs were a prominent family in the village. When the vicar retired, he built a house, Matfield Gate, opposite the vicarage. His widow now lived in it with three unmarried daughters, Miss Freda, Miss May and Miss Amy. The new vicar, a mild unmarried man and his two unmarried sisters, one, Miss Agnes, a talented amateur photographer, were almost literally overlooked by Mrs Storr. Whether he wanted advice or not, he

30

was given it; and every aspect of parish activities were subject to her scrutiny.

Miss Eleanor and Miss Selina Storr, cousins, lived in a large house, Matfield Court, beside the village green. Miss Selina was a brisk walker and in a pork-pie hat and tweed coat and skirt was often to be seen on the road between the village shops and Matfield Court. Miss Eleanor used a bicycle, very large, with a basket in front and a mackintosh guard over the chain. She was known as 'the grenadier' from her upright position as she rode the bicycle.

Matfield in 1916, and for the next decade, was a quiet village. Horses drawing farm carts with loads of hay and ponies and traps were more common traffic than cars. Eileen's pekinese lay in the middle of the road outside the gate, rising to bark if he heard the rumble of cart wheels or the snort of horses.

The main road to the village, half a mile from The Rosery, ran past some cottages, then the gateway to a big Elizabethan manor house, Friars, owned around this time by an eccentric elderly widowed lady, Mrs Minshull. She was not seen in the village, her excursions from Friars limited to sedate drives in her chauffeur-driven limousine. She gave occasional buffet supper parties at which she spoke kindly to Wilfred and Eileen. Wilfred liked her because she had read the novels of Thomas Hardy and was willing to discuss them with him. Eileen felt sorry for her because she lived alone, except for the servants. Her only relative, a nephew, with hair as red as Mrs Minshull's must once have been, visited Friars only occasionally.

The first shop in the village was a confectioner's, a few hundred yards beyond Friars. It had a grey slate pitched roof. Inside, there was room for no more than three customers whose entry to the shop was signalled by a bell ringing in the living room of the cottage behind the shop. Sweets were served with a scoop from large glass jars filled with striped bull's-eyes, pear drops, barley sugar, coconut toffees and other unwrapped sweets.

Cottages, called Chapel Row, stood beside the confectioner's and at the end, Ebenezer, the Baptist chapel. At the time Wilfred and Eileen came to The Rosery it was almost hidden behind tall yew trees, its peaked grey front stained by many years of winter weather. In front of it lay the little graveyard. Eileen, in the early months, used to shudder as she passed its melancholy reminder of mortality. The aged grey stones bore biblical names. Some of the graves had iron railings, rusty and broken. It was not well cared-for; no-one had been buried there for a long time. One large gravestone dominated all others. Leaning slightly, perhaps unsettled by the roots of a yew tree, it bore the inscription 'In loving remembrance of Zippor Buggs 1880'.

Beyond Ebenezer, the road ran beside the village green. The Wheelwright Arms stood on the left hand side, with the forge nearby. The large chestnut tree, shading the open entrance to the forge, had been planted before Oliver Goldsmith was born. A narrow road ran in a semi-circle round the green, past Matfield Court, a 19th-century bay-windowed house, home of the Misses Storr. Then, similar to The Rosery but larger, stood Glenmead, the home of Hinton, Vaughan, Cecil and Katie Castle.

The brothers Castle and their sister had never married. Vaughan, Hinton and Cecil were good-looking, affable men and Eileen sometimes wondered why they had not looked for wives. Calm and unemotional, they liked women well enough but were too comfortable in one another's company to want change. They were not born to strive, and they did not. A good income and a quiet life were theirs. For feminine influence they had their sister Katie, fussy and kind. She called on Eileen and endeared herself by praising Wilfred's gallantry and courage. Eileen knew the Castles were comfortably off, and thought the best answer to Katie's sighs about the rising prices of food and the difficulty of making ends meet was to ask her why she had to try! Katie seemed more puzzled than hurt and, as Eileen told Wilfred later, she went away looking thoughtful.

Miss Childs, the dressmaker, and her aged father had a cottage on the green next door to Hatherleigh, not yet occupied by the Sassoons, who a few years later were to become Wilfred and Eileen's dear friends. On round the green and Maycotts came into view where lived Major Victor Hoare, a bachelor. On the third side of the green was Matfield House, a Georgian edifice, with long windows looking onto a lawn, flanked by iron railings and gate. It had a courtyard on the side, with a clocktower on the outbuildings. Outside the gates were a row of little cottages, two of which were converted to house the village fire-engine.

Some years later one of these cottages was to be occupied by Wilfred's old nurse, Nurse Carter, whose son Wilfred became chauffeur to the family at Matfield House.

Matfield Green, as Siegfried Sassoon wrote in *The Old Century* (his autobiography), had once been used for village cricket matches. But that was before the First World War. The War took the men who had mowed and tended the grass away from the village, and in 1916 it was little more than a field. The pond on the side nearest the village was always a muddy brown but mallards still skimmed it, sometimes staying a few days before they flew on. Once, to Wilfred's delight, they built a nest and hatched a family which made a fine sight as they swam round the pond.

In a cottage, the other side of the main road, lived Mr Owles, who owned a laundry. There were a series of poles on the green outside his cottage gate, and on Mondays he rigged up lines between them. By eleven o'clock, or earlier, combinations, drawers, petticoats, nightshirts, towels and sheets from almost every house in the village were flapping in the breeze. Eileen decided not to use Mr Owles' laundry after she heard a group of village children discussing in less than respectful terms the ownership of some of the undergarments displayed. Some of the washing at The Rosery was done by Clara; sheets and towels were sent to a Tunbridge Wells laundry. They were collected in a large wicker basket and returned, smelling delicious, wrapped in blue tissue paper.

The butcher, Mr Chacksfield, in blue apron and straw hat, was pleased to deal with The Rosery custom from his shop, which had big windows and striped blinds, next door to the Star Hotel. The Star's accommodation was very limited but, as Wilfred found when he was able to walk as far as the village, its bar was used by gentlemen in the village, whereas the Wheelwright Arms, the Standings Cross and the Walnut Tree were frequented by agricultural labourers and tradesmen. Wilfred rather despised this social corralling but, as he was anxious to embrace village life whatever its shortcomings, he in these early years made no attempt to breach tradition by ordering a pint in the Wheelwrights.

Opposite Mr Chacksfield's shop was Newbolds' Grocery and Provision Stores. Eileen and Wilfred discussed which of the three grocery shops they would patronise and decided it would have to be Miss Reeves. Loyalty demanded it, since she had sold them The Rosery. Both Wilfred and Eileen, unused to village life, thought it amazing that such a small village should have three grocery shops. Youngs, the third, also sold newspapers, and Eileen, at Wilfred's behest, wrote a note ordering *The Times* daily.

Miss Reeves' shop was one of two leading off a raised platform or pavement with a wooden roof over it. Ovendens, the bakers, were next door, and for twenty years a slab of cherry madeira cake was delivered every week to The Rosery.

Miss Reeves was a regular attender and supporter of Ebenezer and, in later years, donated a piece of land opposite her shop for a new large red-brick Ebenezer. Strict nonconformist though she was, Miss Reeves did not include among her principles adherence to the Shop Hours Act. There were a number of wooden boxes outside the back door of her shop and a telephone call at any time — except Sunday — would enable a customer to pick up a forgotten or unexpected requirement.

Miss Reeves' shop had two counters, one for drapery and haberdashery, the other for groceries and household necessaries. From the ceiling hung other items — saucepans, kettles, galoshes, wellington boots, doormats and coal scuttles. At Christmas time, a few toys and decorations would be placed in the window, an enticing attraction to the village children who had never seen a toy shop.

Paraffin was also sold. The village had no gas or electricity, so oil lamps and primus stoves were in every house. The Rosery had three oil lamps; one hung from the kitchen ceiling and two others, Alladin lamps with mantles, sat on the tables in the drawing room. Miss Reeves measured paraffin at the back of the shop from a large drum with a tap. Eileen thought that the groceries occasionally had a smell or flavour of paraffin, but Miss Reeves was a stern, unsmiling lady with an air of rectitude which made complaint impossible. Furthermore, there was no rivalry between the shops. Each had its regular customers. Mrs Newbold or Mrs Young would have been astonished if Eileen had appeared on the other side of their counters.

In 1916 the front parlour of a tiny house between Miss Reeves and Youngs was the Matfield Sub-Post Office. As in the confectioners and the bakers, the bell rang in the parlour when a customer opened the door.

Miss Simpson lived in a white cottage (always called 'Miss Simpson's') next to Mr Owles' laundry, opposite the pond. She was often seen, busy gardening, within her white paling fence and gate. She was a friend of Miss Muriel Stagg, a neighbour of Wilfred and Eileen. The two ladies lived together for a time while Miss Stagg's new house, Whiteholme, was built in Foxhole Lane.

Miss Simpson was twenty, or even thirty, years older than Eileen. But it was not easy to tell the ages of the spinster ladies of Matfield, for they all dressed in 'sensible' clothes which were not youthful in colour nor style.

Miss Simpson owned a bicycle and rode it much faster than Miss Eleanor Storr and other lady cyclists in Matfield. In Wilfred's and Eileen's early years in Matfield, the only considerable danger on the road was Wilfred's pony and trap. But, early in the 'thirties, there were buses and more cars on the road. One morning, Miss Simpson was pedalling furiously in a high wind which blotted out the sound of an approaching car as she swerved off the highway towards her house. The car ran straight into the bicycle and she was killed instantly. Miss Simpson was mourned by people who had liked, even loved, her in the houses of the village, big and small. I remember hearing, as a little girl, a conversation about the accident which referred to 'a marvellous way to go'. My imagination had presented me with a grim picture of Miss Simpson flying through the air surrounded by bits of her bicycle; I couldn't believe that such an awful event was in any way 'marvellous'!

Eileen's ownership of a pekinese brought about an early visit to The Rosery of the Misses Beech, sisters who lived in a Georgian village house in Paddock Wood. Paddock Wood had a railway station, the nearest to Matfield, and some three miles distant. The Misses Beech had an unusual tandem tricycle with a big basket in front for their two pekineses. They stoically pushed this contraption up the steep, long Gedges Hill, past Weirleigh, the home of old Mrs Sassoon, mother of Siegfried. They pedalled triumphantly through Matfield village to The Rosery, their pekineses looking over the top of the basket, perhaps anticipating anxiously their meeting with Chou.

Goldfinches and Thistle

3 – EARLY DAYS

A difference over prayer – Tommy the Welsh pony – the fox-hunt – a late war casualty – conflict of impatience and gratitude – the New Testament.

All his sufferings, physical disabilities and grief at the casualty lists, which continued to bring news of the loss of many friends and contemporaries at school, Cambridge and London Rifle Brigade, had not lessened Wilfred's Christianity nor his patriotism. He was disappointed that Eileen did not share his fondness for and belief in prayer. When he urged her to kneel with him and pray at bedtime, she would not, and when, disappointed, he pressed her she said, 'I prayed all the time you were out at the front and when you were in hospital. And you know your mother was going to churches and getting them to pray for you. She even made you go to church in a bath chair and give thanks. It didn't do any good'.

'Eileen, that's blasphemous,' Wilfred reproached her. 'Doesn't it strike you we have to thank God I'm alive and we are able to live together, happily?'

'No, I think it's a shame,' she blurted out. Then, seeing the fear and concern on his face, she put her hands in front of her eyes. He knelt down and prayed for her, but he had to accept that Eileen, so compliant and anxious to please him in everything else, could not share his religious fervor. The real reason was that coupled with her disinterest in Christianity was a superstitious dread of any discussion of death or illness.

As the months passed, Wilfred's willpower and physical strength gradually overcame his difficulty in walking. He practised walking without a stick and, although he often fell over, which worried Eileen, he was determined to achieve his goal. He could now use his left hand to do much of the work of his useless right hand. He noted with scientific curiosity that his writing looked quite different, as if another person had used the pen. He

37

could read for much longer periods, but Eileen knew it tired him and would read aloud for hours every evening. She had a beautiful voice, one which never tired or faltered, and Wilfred would lie back in his big arm chair with his eyes closed listening to the classical writers whose work he had always admired but of late years had had no time to read.

There was then no bus to Tunbridge Wells. To visit villages and country around which Wilfred longed to explore, he thought a pony and trap would give him freedom of movement. He broached the idea to Eileen. As he had expected, she resisted it, complaining that it was far too dangerous for him to drive with one hand, and she knew he wouldn't let her drive for him. As he argued, he began to repeat words, which Eileen knew was a sign of strain. Abruptly, she agreed.

So for £20 they bought a shaggy, fat Welsh pony which the vet assured them was sound in wind and limb. A cream-coloured governess cart, harness and stable furnishings cost almost as much. For a few shillings a week, an ex-serviceman, Corporal Floyd, living in the village, agreed to help with the grooming and care of the pony.

Soon after Corporal Floyd began his duties, he suggested that Tommy was clipped all over, which smartened his appearance. Plenty of oats and good grooming and Tommy's docile character changed. From being a quiet, slow pony, he became restless, stubborn and fast if it pleased him. The trap now bowled through the village at a spanking pace, and only the almost empty highways, comparatively free of traffic, prevented the turnout being a menace to all on the roads. Tommy was also unpredictable, sometimes stopping and turning round at the sight of a traction engine or a steam toller. He also developed a mischievous streak. Once, perhaps sensing that, with one hand, Wilfred could not hold him and dry him after a wet ride, he turned his head and gave him a sharp nip on the behind, which left a bruise for weeks.

However Tommy made expeditions possible. One of these was to a meet of the nearest foxhounds. It was a seven miles drive before they came to the meet, but the sun shone, pale and clear out of a winter sky, and the air was crisp, with enough breeze to dry the roads. By the time they arrived, Eileen was too cold to pretend to any enthusiasm. Moreover, she had told Wilfred that she didn't want to see the kill for, she said, 'I can't stand the idea of killing anything, more especially now because of the War'. Although Wilfred shared her feeling, he was anxious to follow the hounds by driving along the road, skirting the wood where they were now giving tongue. Riders began to gallop down the adjoining field.

'No, darling, you promised me we shouldn't follow', pleaded Eileen. Wilfred gave in with a bad grace, turning the pony round and hitting him with the whip so that he broke into a gallop. In this way, Wilfred sulking and Eileen tearful, they careered down the road until they approached The Rosery.

This was the last time they ever went to a meet.

They kept Tommy for a few more years. Finally he was sold because they could no longer afford the extra expense. Meanwhile he developed a habit of stopping outside every public house in the village and demanded a lot of coaxing before he would move on. Wilfred concluded that he had become accustomed to these stops when Corporal and Mrs Floyd borrowed him, as they were allowed to do, when he was not required.

Exasperating though Tommy was, Wilfred was fond of him and anxious when he developed a small tumour on his jaw, which ulcerated. The vet said it must be cut out and cauterised.

Wilfred drove Tommy into Tunbridge Wells for the operation one morning, and was dismayed that the vet took none of the steps that could avoid inflicting suffering. Tommy was immobilised by means of a twitch: a cord noose slipped over the upper lip, by the nostril and inside the mouth against the gums, and tightened up by twisting it with a short pole until the lip resembled a ball and the animal's eyes were wide, staring with distress. Then while his assistant held the twitch, the vet neatly cut out the lump and seared the hole with a red hot iron.

After an hour Wilfred drove the dispirited Tommy home, allowing him to meander, his wound still dripping, and failing, as he usually did, to cut a dash through Matfield.

Wilfred one day drove out to a nearby military hospital to see an old friend who had served in his regiment, promoted to captain, but who had been invalided out when his leg had been shattered by a bullet. Now he was under the care of a Colonel in the R.A.M.C. who had taught Wilfred at Cambridge and of whose competence Wilfred had a poor opinion.

Wilfred found his friend, sitting in a wheel chair, his leg up, his face pale. He was pleased to see Wilfred but did not want to talk about the War, and especially not about the fighting. This was common, as Wilfred noted; few who had experienced the horror of the front line wanted to recall it.

The wounded man complained bitterly of his medical treatment. 'I don't want any of the wounded hero stuff,' he said, 'but the Colonel treats us as if we were a lot of criminals. He comes round in the morning, swaggering and laughing. He doesn't wash his hands, probes a wound or squeezes another, alters the position of a broken limb so roughly that some shout or faint. What's more, I know I haven't been treated correctly. My leg was going on alright until it was operated on six weeks ago and it's been full of pus ever since'.

Wilfred didn't know what to say, for he thought from his friend's sickly appearance that he would have to lose the leg if his life were to be saved. He comforted him as well as he could, at the same time urging him to ask for a transfer to a London hospital. Full of foreboding, he said good-bye and went to fetch Tommy.

Three weeks later Wilfred heard that the leg had been amputated, but it was too late. His friend died, one of the many who survived only to die in hospital. Wilfred thought yet again, as he had often done, that but for Eileen's determination to move him from a military hospital to the London Hospital he also would have died.

He thought of the aspects of his life which led him to thank God nightly: that he had survived, and would live on into the peaceful years which were sure to come. His love for Eileen and hers for him were central to his happiness. He resolved to curb the impatient words he sometimes uttered which he knew upset her. He did not underestimate the difficulty he would have in controlling the frustrations which often led him to berate her, without fault though she was. He always asked her forgiveness after he had been unkind (as he thought), and she gave it more to comfort him than because she thought it was necessary. She understood him perfectly, and loved him so much that Wilfred sometimes worried that such dedication was idolatrous, perhaps standing in the way of love of God that he longed for her to experience. But this thought he did not pursue for fear it would lead him to further criticism of her which he had now determined to root out.

The tragic death of his friend drew him to a deeper study of Christian teaching in the hope that there lay the solution that would end the slaughter by human beings of one another. Reading the New Testament every day comforted him. He read and re-read the sermons and addresses of Bishop Barnes of Birmingham, whom he had known at Cambridge. Bishop Barnes was a theologian who believed in the work of Darwin on the origin of man and sought to reconcile it with the teachings of Christ. Wilfred found his writings strongly compatible with his own beliefs.

4 – ILLNESS

*Diabetes – a false alarm – Susie Willett's antagonism –
rejoicing – depression at loss of medical career.*

Wilfred was an early riser. On a chilly September morning he
was busy hoeing the rosebeds when Johnson, the postman, came
up the path. Johnson was always ready for a gossip. Wilfred
stood talking to him for ten mintues after which he noticed his
left foot getting cold – the right foot, of course, he could not feel.
So wishing Johnson good morning he went into the house and
called Clara to bring his breakfast.

He could not rid himself of the chilled feeling. By the evening
he had a headache, internal pains and a high temperature. Eileen
insisted on sending for the doctor. For a week he lay in bed,
meekly taking all the medicines prescribed by the doctor and
gradually feeling the weakness subsiding.

One day, however, the doctor sat by his bed looking
unusually serious and, after some inconsequential talk, blurted
out: 'I am afraid I have found sugar in your urine'.

This was before the discovery of insulin. Diabetes meant a
slow death.

Wilfred, who was just beginning to enjoy life a little, found it
hard to think that fate, or God as he thought, had struck him
down. Rallying from the shock, and struggling for calm, he said,
'Perhaps it is on account of my brain injury? I think sugar
appears in the urine of dogs after certain cerebal lesions'.

'Yes, yes, very likely. Just take it easy and try not to worry. It's
probably only a temporary condition that will clear up.' So
saying, he took his departure, avoiding Wilfred's eyes.

When the doctor had gone, Eileen wanted to know what he
had said. Fortunately she did not know how fatal diabetes was in
a young adult. Wilfred held her hand all that night as though it
were only through her that he kept his touch on earth.

For the next three weeks he went about pretending to take an interest in the garden, knowing it to be a pretence. Soon he would be too weak to do anything. It was never out of his thoughts, and every thought ended in silent prayer that God would allow him to recover.

Eileen saw that he was not recovering from illness as quickly as she hoped. Unusually for her, she sought her mother-in-law's advice. Mrs Willett made immediate arrangements for him to see a consultant physician with a good reputation who had recently come to Tunbridge Wells.

Mrs Willett said that Wilfred had better stay at The Homestead for the night before the appointment: it would be more restful for him. She did not, however, invite Eileen. When Wilfred asked if she could come too, he was told that the maids might give notice if asked to do any extra work.

As Wilfred sat in the leather armchair in the morning room of The Homestead, it seemed to him that the past years had never happened:

'Dinner is at the usual time, Wilfred,' said his mother. 'But you needn't change if you're tired. Your father will forgive you, I know. Just lift your head.' She smiled as she straightened the monogrammed head cover of the armchair.

'Oh that's all right Mater, I'd like to change'.

As he was shown into his bedroom, a fire glowing in the grate, his case unpacked and his evening clothes spread on the bed, Wilfred had the feeling that his mother wanted to show him what comforts he was missing, now that he was married. After dinner, as he sat round the drawing room fire with his parents, he felt it might be the last time he would be with them without their knowledge of his illness. So, after a reflective silence, he said:

'Mater, I want you to forgive Eileen and me. I know you didn't want us to marry, but if you only knew how kind and good she is and how happy she makes me, I am sure you would have asked her to stay'.

'Wilfred, I do hope you are not going to make a scene,' interrupted his mother. His father rose and patted him kindly on the back muttering, 'There, there, old man, there's no need to be histrionic'.

Wilfred never again asked his mother to show Eileen any affection.

Next morning, he was ready and waiting when Eileen called to go with him to see the doctor.

'You look very well,' he was told as he entered the consulting room. The doctor had taken the trouble to get his notes from the London Hospital as well as from the Matfield doctor.

'Now, let's see you walk,' he said.

Wilfred limped up and down the room.

'Splendid, splendid,' he squeaked, for he had a high pitched little voice, 'You walk with a rhythm now, a splendid recovery. Now what's this about sugar . . .?'

He went off with a specimen; soon he returned. 'Exactly,' he beamed, 'as I thought, no trace of sugar, and never has been. Your country doctor doesn't keep his Fehling's solution freshly made up. I wonder you didn't suspect it. You remember, phosphates will precipitate Fehling's if it's an old solution.'

The return to The Rosery was joyful. Wilfred now could explain to Eileen all his fears of dying. She wept as she held him in her arms in their bedroom at The Rosery, beseeching him never to hide anything from her again.

The relief, the gladness, that Wilfred felt that he was not mortally ill was short-lived, as such emotion usually is. Before long he was plunged into one of the depressions which occurred intermittently, with more or less severity, for the rest of his life. Sometimes these were transitory. Less frequently, they lasted for weeks, sapping his energy and requiring all Eileen's strength and love as she struggled to lift his spirits. This time the cause was the anguish he still felt, perhaps always would feel although in diminishing degree, that he had not been able to practise medicine. He knew that diabetes was one of the many unsolved problems that had fascinated him at the London Hospital. Scientist and idealist, he had dreamed of involvement in the advances in medical knowledge which he knew would come. He believed he had stood on the threshold of important medical discoveries, but that fate had robbed him of the power to use the innate faculties that could have led him to their achievement for mankind.

44

5 — THE FIRST CHILD

Fear of impotence — Miss Stagg — breech birth —
superstition — Nannie Read.

In the early summer of 1917 Eileen told Wilfred joyfully that, at
last, she was pregnant. She knew that, despite the doctors'
reassurances, he had blamed himself for her failure to conceive.
His resolute mind looked forward to the possibilities for
achievement in his life which lay ahead, and he never allowed
himself to regret his damaged body. Nevertheless to be deprived
of fatherhood was a thought so bitter that he had tried not to
contemplate it. Now the anxiety was over.

Wilfred proudly told his parents the news. Despite remarks
about another mouth to feed on his limited resources, they were
pleased. His younger brother, Lewis, who was in the Black
Watch, had married a women older than himself and there were
as yet no children.

Before many weeks had passed Eileen was prostrate. Nausea
wracked her from the time she got up in the morning until
evening. Never had she felt so wretched. To add to her misery,
Wilfred became short-tempered. He was accustomed to her help
with the things he could still not manage to do with one hand,
but now whenever she moved she was sick. Try though he did to
suppress his irritation and frustration, it burst through several
times a day. He was always penitent, but she was often in tears.

Eileen's patience with Wilfred was thought remarkable by
their next-door neighbour, Miss Muriel Stagg, who lived with
her elderly mother at The Pines, separated from The Rosery by a
field.

Miss Stagg was an unusually gifted gardener. All day she
laboured to produce beautiful flowers and fine vegetables; and
when she was not working she was reading about them. In the
tense months before the baby's birth she sought to occupy
Wilfred by teaching him how to plant and grow for the best

results. She would come down to The Rosery and help him prepare beds. She would go with him to nurseries to choose roses and plants for the herbacious borders. She was a true friend.

When at last the nine months were up, the longed-for baby's arrival in the world in their bedroom at The Rosery was a traumatic experience. For four days Eileen screamed in intermittent agony as the doctor, summoned from Tunbridge Wells, and the monthly maternity nurse struggled to help her with a breech birth. Wilfred spent most of the time on his knees, praying in the drawing room, in the dining room, even in the kitchen as he boiled some water on the primus stove, Clara having let the kitchen range go out, so flustered was she at the drama being enacted in the bedroom over the kitchen.

Eileen was the centre of Wilfred's life. Without her, in his crippled state, he thought it would be impossible for him to carry on an independent existence. Strongly as he desired a child, and so he knew, did she, all he cared for as he stood outside the bedroom door on the fourth day was her survival.

Suddenly, he heard what seemed to be a gull's cry, far off in the wind. His heart throbbed strongly as he realised the child was born. Some minutes later the doctor came out and, smiling, said that a boy had been born and both were all right.

'But it was touch and go,' he added, 'whether we could ever bring the child round. He was white. Never seen the cord so tight round the neck of a child, looped round and strangling him. It took twenty minutes before he started to breathe. I nearly gave it up.

When the monthly nurse left, Eileen found it difficult to give Wilfred the devoted care she still thought he needed as well as caring for the infant.

She was able to feed him and was never happier than cradling him in her arms as Wilfred sat by her, holding the baby's tiny hand in his. He was to be christened 'Denis Gerald'. Wilfred had had a friend called Gerard who had been killed in the war and wanted to call his son after him, but Eileen objected. She has always been superstitious and even more so since Wilfred had been wounded on December 13. So Wilfred agreed that 'Gerald' should be substituted for 'Gerard'.

When Eileen's mother and stepfather Munt drove from London to see the baby, Mrs Munt offered to pay for a nannie for Denis. Eileen gratefully accepted the offer and Nannie Read arrived at The Rosery. She was about thirty. She had lost her mother when she was still a child. When her father married again she had fallen out with her stepmother and moved to London, first as a nurserymaid and then as a nannie. She had lost touch with her own family and, as was then customary with nannies, she identified herself wholly with the family she served. Her one friend in the world was another nannie. They had met when they were both nurserymaids in a large family.

Domestic staff in those days did not have much time off — one day a month was usual. Women, especially, had little opportunity for marriage unless they were fortunate enough to meet partners in the households in which they served. Thus, although Nannie had a trim figure and a pleasant face, she had never had a 'follower', as a suitor would have been called. By the time she came to The Rosery, she no longer expected ever to have children of her own.

Nannie had a large capacity for love and gave it to her charges. But it was never expressed in the warmth of hugs and kisses. This would not have been within the 'nannie' tradition. She showed it by a minute attention to the care of babies and little children, by sharp admonition where she thought it necessary, and by unselfish 'treats' bought with her own careful savings. She never smacked a child.

What she didn't understand was that money was not plentiful at The Rosery. Luxuries like marmet prams, repainting nurseries, or nursery maids were anxiously discussed by Wilfred and Eileen. Wilfred felt harassed when he had to refuse Nannie's demands; and she would sulk.

Nannie would have been more comfortable in the wealthy family she moved on to after nine years; but it was The Rosery family who looked after her in her old age.

6 — PEACE

German offensive — 'backs to the wall' — Armistice —
Spanish 'flu — Memorial — contention — church v. chapel —
Eileen and Poppy Day.

The months that followed the birth of Denis were a time of
happiness and fulfilment for Wilfred. Yet often he felt guilty. The
war was not going well for England. He believed he had no right
to be happy when many of his fellow countrymen were fighting
and dying. General Ludendorff's offensive in March 1918
lasted four long months. On 12 April Sir Douglas Haig issued
his Order of the Day: 'With our backs to the wall and believing
in the justice of our cause, each one of us must fight to
the end'.

Wilfred's anxiety was not shared by Eileen. She was
preoccupied with the baby and had ceased to attend church
services. Wilfred's greatest source of comfort was to kneel with
other members of the congregation in Matfield church to pray
for victory and that the French army, 'our gallant allies', would
hold out. It was not until August that the British Fourth Army
broke through German lines, turning the tide of battle.

At 11 a.m. on 11 November the First World War came to an
end.

That afternoon Wilfred walked to the village. He wanted to
see the flags flying and the preparations for the bonfire on the
green. He met Miss Selina Storr and was embarrassed but
pleased when she clasped both hands round his useless right
one and with tears in her eyes said, 'Mr Willett, we all owe you so
much'. He wanted to demur, to deprecate, to tell her that
nothing was owed to him whose life had been preserved but
everything was owed to the millions of Englishmen who had not
survived. But the words would not come. The tears that he could
not now control gathered in his eyes and fell on her hands.

Before the winter had passed, the Spanish influenza epidemic swept the world. Millions died. When the first case appeared in Matfield, Eileen was distraught. Strangely, those most vulnerable to the unidentified but sinister virus were the young and strong. When Mr Ovenden's daughter died, aged 18, Eileen besought Wilfred to stop going to the village, to stop going to church. She worried that the maids would bring infection into the house. She couldn't stop them visiting their families but she told them they mustn't go into The Rosery nursery. She served Wilfred's food herself so that his contact with them was minimal. Wilfred was tolerant of Eileen's behaviour. He had the fatalism of one who had lately survived death. She had the sharpened fears of one who had nearly lost a beloved being.

The winter seemed endless. Another young girl, the daughter of the Podmores of Moatlands, died. Moatlands was a Victorian mansion between Paddock Wood and Matfield, surrounded by acres of land and water. Yet the infection had crept into this prosperous household.

By spring 1919, the influenza epidemic had waned. Eileen was pregnant again. The new baby would be born in October and Eileen's mother and father insisted that she should have it at Ashburn Place under the care of a specialist.

She suffered much less discomfort in this second pregnancy and when the vicar, Mr Tomlinson, called a parish meeting to discuss the Memorial to the men from Matfield village who had died on active service, she told Wilfred she would go along with him. It was July 1919.

Wilfred had thought about it for some months. Many of the young men he had laughed and played with, who should have been life-time friends, lay beneath the soil of France, killed at Passchendaele, on the Somme, or in the weary and futile trench warfare.

Wilfred rose to his feet at the beginning of the meeting. His speech hesitation, from which he had never recovered, was particularly frustrating to him on an occasion when he wished to be impressive and to express deeply-felt opinions:

'I think we should buy a field as near the centre of the village as we can', he began. 'Build a small wooden pavilion for changing in; have a cricket pitch for which our village green is unsuitable; swings and seats for the children and all round the ground plant oak trees for each man from Matfield killed in the war; put a brass plate by each tree with the name of the man. Then there will be a living memorial to each man that his children and his family can be proud of, to play round when young or sit under its shade as they grow older.'

There was silence for a few minutes. Then Mr Tomlinson asked if anyone would second the proposal; again silence.

Eileen glanced indignantly round the hall, as Wilfred resumed his seat, his lip quivering, as she saw apprehensively. How could such stupid people, as she now thought those with whom she had been on the friendliest terms yesterday, turn down Wilfred's splendid idea? She had read endlessly from the war poets to him. Although she had, sooner than he, rejected Rupert Brooke's glorious enthusiasm for a patriotic war and found herself agreeing with the mordant brilliance of Wilfred Owen and others, she longed now to forget about death and would prefer living, growing trees to the sad and melancholy granite cross, engraved with the names of the dead, which was finally decided on.

Mr Punnett, the builder, had made an alternative suggestion: a village hall, which he would not only build at cost price but give £20 towards. This caused the chimney sweep to jump up and declare, 'That'll be used for dancing and all kinds of Devil's carryings-on. Is that a decent memorial for my boy that was always God-fearing and now lies buried in France!' Tears streamed down his face and Mr Punnett said hastily, 'Of course, I only suggested a hall as a fitting memorial, and it's for the meeting to decide. But do what you like, you'll never be able to keep young people from enjoying themselves'.

'No, and I don't want to: but there's a joy in God if we don't put temptations in their way!'

'And I, as an old man, can say he is right,' added one of the churchwardens.

'Well,' Mr Tomlinson, the vicar and chairman of the meeting hastily and nervously interjected, 'a cross on the village green seems a very appropriate suggestion to me.'

'Far better to place it in the House of God, our village church', the churchwarden answered.

'I object to that,' said Mr Baldock, one-man farmer, 'Just as many of our boys from the chapel gave their lives. And you know we don't hold with a cross at all for the memorial. You can't expect us chapel folk to subscribe. I suppose you'll want to pass the hat round before you've done.'

After another hour of dispute it was decided to fill up a pond by the church and erect a cross on the site. Wilfred was gratified to find that he was proposed and seconded to serve on the organising committee. The site belonged to a retired business man who had owned the land on which the church had been built. He graciously presented the pond to the village, thereby ridding himself of a stagnant nuisance about which the Rural Council constantly complained. Mr Marchant, a landowner whose family owned and had built Matfield House, offered to provide the earth to fill it in free if he could be paid for the labour and cartage. The committee sanctioned the payment to him of £100. A stock granite memorial cross, one of the thousands erected at that time in villages and towns all over the British Isles, was purchased for a cost of £250. Everyone in Matfield subscribed. Out of a total of £500 enough was left to buy a mower to cut the grass when it grew round the memorial and to insure the structure against lightning. A memorial tablet was somehow squeezed in for the church, but not for the chapel.

On the day it was unveiled by the Conservative Member of Parliament for Tunbridge Wells, all who had served in the forces paraded in uniform, wearing their medals. Wilfred was proud of his Mons Star with bar and the oak leaves, denoting a mention in dispatches, on the Victory ribbon. Eileen never saw those medals, which Wilfred was to wear on every Armistice Sunday, without reflecting at what cost they had been won. However, once when his mother said it was a pity Wilfred hadn't waited to qualify in medicine so that he could have gone into the R.A.M.C. as a major, Eileen retorted sharply that in that event he would probably have been killed on the Somme. This outburst was unusual, for she habitually bore such taunts in silence.

51

Wilfred's disappointment at the rejection of his imaginative idea for a memorial to Matfield's war dead was short-lived. He was consoled by the part he had played in organising the erection of the memorial, and was relieved that one of the obsolete army tanks, which were distributed to towns and villages throughout Britain as a grisly memorial of the War, was not deposited in Matfield. Tunbridge Wells had several, one remaining on the triangular green near the Vale Road Post Office until late in the 'thirties.

Sometime later, 11 November, Armistice Day, was designated 'Poppy Day'. Disabled ex-servicemen made poppies which were sold for their benefit. Someone suggested it would be fitting for Eileen to organise this charitable event in Matfield. She agreed to please Wilfred and did it, without enjoyment and haphazardly, for the rest of her life. Big boxes full of poppies were delivered to The Rosery early in November and had to be sorted into trays for the sellers. The result for many days was a chaotic sea of poppies on the drawing room floor.

There was none of the later egalitarianism when every poppy looked the same and people made whatever offering they fancied. Poppies then were 3d, 6d, and 1s; car poppies were half-a-crown. The one-shilling poppies were made of silk and were very fine. Wilfred always wore a three-penny poppy so as not to distinguish himself from 'other ranks' ex-servicemen in the village, but he put more than three pennies in the collecting box.

Village events, like the annual sports on the Green, Bonfire Night and Armistice Day, loomed large in the life of Matfield villagers because in the early 1920's there were few other distractions apart from births, marriages and deaths. And there were not many of them. The Church Registers of the period are remarkably slim volumes.

On Armistice Day, survivors of the War assembled on the Green for the march to the War Memorial where a service was held. Wilfred limped beside the small column. All wore their medals on their Sunday suits, with a poppy in their buttonholes. As the years went by, fewer gathered on the Green. Wilfred, on Eileen's insistence, would join the march outside The Rosery so that he had a shorter distance to walk.

7 – MARJORIE

Church and civil names – the outhouse – pears and butterflies – abortive seedlings – fishing with father – hops and the oasthouse – from Tiger Tim *to* Children's Newspaper *– Denis and boats.*

Early in October my mother and father moved into Ashburn Place with my grandparents and a monthly nurse to await the birth. Denis was left at The Rosery with Nannie.

My father had hoped for a boy and was disappointed when he was told he had a daughter. The birth this time was without drama, except that my mother complained that the baby could have been born quarter of an hour earlier if the nurse hadn't held it back so that it could be born in the presence of the consultant whose arrival had been delayed. Quite how the nurse had achieved this extraordinary feat was never explained to my satisfaction when I was old enough to be curious about the circumstances of my birth.

It was customary for mothers to stay in bed for three weeks after a birth but my father was restless, longing to see if the apples had been picked and correctly stored at The Rosery. So he hired a car and, despite my grandmother's lamentations, mother and baby were packed into it and I was given into Nannie's care in the rose-patterned nursery above the porch.

My birth certificate tells me that I was registered in London as 'Audrey Marjorie'. This small detail was forgotten eight weeks later when I was christened at Matfield Church 'Marjorie Suzanne', the new name a concession to my Grandmother Susie Willett and also, I presume, to the Huguenot ancestors. Re-registration would have cost my parents only five shillings, but they must have considered it unimportant for it was not until my father gave me my birth certificate when I was 16 that I discovered my legal first names.

My earliest memory is of climbing out of the huge double

pram, parked at the back door. I must have been two-and-a-half years old then and had heard the unfamiliar sound of an aeroplane.

My final memory of that big double pram is the old coal house roof collapsing on top of it some time during the Second World War. Why it was kept, gradually decaying and covered in coal dust, remains a mystery. The most likely explanation is simply that my mother thought it might come in useful one day.

The coal house was part of the outbuildings some ten yards from the back door. In between the house and the outbuildings was a paved yard on which, in their first years at The Rosery, stood my father's trap. Next to the coal house was the stable (later the garage), wherein also in the early years dwelled the pony, Tommy. Next to the stable and the coal house was a building known as the outhouse, and above the stable and the outhouse were two rooms reached by a ladder which, as I remember, stopped somewhat short of the opening to the upper storey. My brother and I became adept at hauling ourselves up by an iron ring sunk into the wall, into the mysterious rooms aloft.

The most attractive objects in these disused tack rooms were two large black leather trunks, one with E.E.J.S. stamped in gold (Eileen Estelle Josephine Stenhouse) and the other with W.L.W. (Wilfred Leslie Willett). The contents of these trunks, which we constantly dragged out even as they gradually disintegrated, were old skirts and blouses which must have belonged to my mother as a girl, a collection of old shoes and boots and pieces of a khaki uniform, including a brown belt with mildew on it, and a leather-covered flask. As I remember, the excursions aloft gradually became dangerous as some of the floor boards began to rot. On one occasion I was nearly precipitated into the outhouse below.

The outbuildings were overshadowed by a large, old pear tree. The pears were green and hard, suitable only for cooking. When they fell, in late September, we had cooked pears every day for pudding. But even so, many were left on the ground and the most beautiful butterflies came and fed off them. The glorious colours of the Red Admirals and the Painted Ladies fascinated me. I saw children on the village green racing to catch them in muslin butterfly nets which Miss Reeves sold. Did my father tell me that it was wrong to end the flutter of those glorious wings? or did it come from within me? Whichever it was, I never killed a butterfly.

My father gave me a small patch of garden under a plum tree and with my pocket money, 3d a week, I bought seed at Miss Reeves. I was always disappointed that the pictures on the little packets did not come to life in my garden. Nannie said that I didn't water the seeds enough; but when I did, many of the little seedlings were washed away. One day Nannie gave me three plants of white 'Mrs Simpkins' pinks. I planted these carefully, pressing the earth in round them with my fingers and was rewarded a few weeks later with some blooms. I didn't pick them but squatted in the middle of my garden enjoying their scent.

My father also gave me a little fishing rod for he had been given special permission by Mr Punnett to fish on Friars Lake, which belonged to Mr Punnett at The Lodge, not far from the church, and not to Mrs Minshull at Friars. Mr Punnett also owned the oasthouse, opposite The Rosery. There was a footpath alongside this which was the beginning of a public right of way through woods and fields to the small village of Petteridge. Sometimes Denis came with our father and me as we walked through Mr Punnett's orchard (by special permission) to reach the dam across the lake. Halfway across the dam, there was a willow tree, and here we put down our rods and baited the hooks, with our father's help, with worms. He was expert at 'casting' with one hand but Denis and I often caught our lines in the willow tree. At last we got the floats in the water at an adequate distance from the bank and sat down to await the exciting moment when the float would bob under and the line reel out as a fish took the bait. The small fish we caught, perch, were slippery and slimy when they were landed on the bank. Sometimes my father carefully took the hooks out of their mouths and threw them back. The sport was the catching, he explained; one should only kill if they were big enough to eat.

In the autumn, a pleasant smell of roasting hops drifted over the road to The Rosery garden. The hops were placed on the upper floor of the oast house and were roasted by furnaces beneath them.

The autumn was also the time for conkers to fall from the row of horse chestnut trees bordering the road on Miss Macfarlane's and Miss Barnes' land at Matfield Grove. The conkers that fell in the road were picked up by the village children, but greatly daring, Denis and I used to climb through a hole in the hedge between The Rosery and The Grove and gather up all the conkers we could see on the inside of the fence, one of us keeping a lookout for Miss Macfarlane. One year I collected them in a cardboard box and buried them as 'treasure'. A few weeks later, when I uncovered the box, I thought that a witch had replaced my shiny conkers with dull brown ones.

Denis was able to read when he was five, and my mother paid 2d a week for *Tiger Tim* to be delivered to The Rosery. We had this comic for two or three years and, when I could read, I was absorbed in the adventures of Mrs Bruin's boys. It was a disappointment when my father replaced *Tiger Tim* with the *Children's Newspaper* which was not in colour and seemed very dull.

A deep ditch which filled with water in winter lay on one side of The Rosery garden, separating it from Mr Lavender's cottage. Denis was always fascinated by boats and water, and occupied himself busily for hours trying to make rafts with his carpentry set.

Denis's wellingtons, always called 'godgers', were often damp from the water which filled them when his rafts sank. I complained, crossly, to Nannie that he was always 'bagging' mine so that neither of us ever had dry boots.

In autumn Denis would light fires and place fallen chestnuts to roast amidst the burning twigs. Black on the outside, cold on the inside, they weren't appetising, but Denis insisted they were full of vitamins. Our father often gave us this kind of nature information, and our general knowledge was wider than that of most other children.

8 — ANNE

*The allowance threatened again — have the baby adopted? —
the solution: an extension — Fred Coles — bricklaying —
strike.*

When I was three-and-a-half, my sister was born. Years later my
mother told me how fearful she was when she had to tell my
grandmother Willett (the forbidding Susie) of her pregnancy.
My parents knew that the tiny additions to his war pension which
my father received both for my brother and for me would not be
granted for any child born after 1919. The allowance of £100
from my grandmother, who completely dominated her
husband, was vital if ends were to be met in household ex-
penditure. There were several occasions when my father was
told by his mother that the allowance would be withdrawn, and
my mother feared that this would be one of them. However,
although severely scolded and advised to have the baby
adopted, the allowance was continued.

My parents thought that The Rosery would be too small
when the third child arrived and that they would have to move, a
decision that would have meant living in Tunbridge Wells. Few
houses at that time came up for sale in Matfield. My mother
dreaded the closer proximity of her domineering mother-in-
law. Moreover, my father had found consolation for his lost
career in medicine by an increasingly scientific interest in
bird life, which abounded in the woods, gardens, ponds and
lakes around Matfield and which he would lose in Tunbridge
Wells.

On an income of £450 a year, he had a man to help him in the
garden and my mother had a nannie and a maid. The gardener,
aged about 50, was a cantankerous countryman called Fred
Coles.

Coles had suggested to my father that they should clear some
shrubs and plant Cox and Bramley apple trees:

'Of course I'd like to do that,' said my father, 'but I don't know whether I shall be able to stop here. You see there's another child coming.' My father did not like telling him, but presumed he must know since Clara knew, and therefore probably the whole village:

'I wondered something of the sort,' said Coles, more embarrassed than my father, 'but why don't you build another room where that side door is?'

'Building costs have gone up since the war', replied my father, irritated by the idea that Coles thought he could afford it on a war pension.

'It wouldn't cost a lot to do it if you did it yourself.'

'But it means all sorts of skilled jobs.'

'Well I built a cottage of my own before the war.'

'Oh yes I forgot you're a bricklayer. But still there must be a lot more as well.'

'Nothing that we couldn't get over.'

Although my father at first dismissed the idea, the more he thought about it, the more he longed to do it. My mother encouraged him, telling him that, if the worst came to the worst, he could always get Mr Punnett, who was a neighbour, and a builder, to finish it.

That evening they went to see the Punnetts. Ethel Punnett had been a kind friend to my mother. She was a few years older and had never fully recovered from the shock of having a still-born baby. She had told my mother that she would never be able to bear a living child. Perhaps as a result of this she had lost interest in her femininity and always wore corduroy breeches and a man's jacket. She had a parrot and four rough-haired terriers on whom she lavished the affection no longer wanted by her husband. There was gossip in the village that he had a woman friend, but Eileen hoped this was not true, for she knew that, although an unhappy marriage was calamitous for a woman, a broken one could be tragic. Especially was this true if a deserted wife had no money. Mrs Punnett had no money of her own, and Eileen and Wilfred thought it unwise that she so often had her impecunious brother, William, to stay. Idle by nature, he would lounge about the Lodge, indulged by his sister, for weeks on end, exasperating Mr Punnett by his presence as well as his fondness for Mr Punnett's whisky.

Fortunately William was not at the Lodge when my parents called to discuss the extension to The Rosery.

Mr Punnett was pleased that my father had come to consult him. He offered to supply a plan for the building and order the rubble, bricks and wall tiles required for the start of the building. My father had decided that there should be two rooms added, a study for himself and a bedroom above it.

The plan arrived in two days. When my father showed it to Coles he did not think much of it, and as the building went up altered it in most particulars. This was confusing to my father, but he had to be guided by a man who had built before and therefore could be presumed to know what he was about. He was entirely under Coles' direction, fetching and carrying, watching to find out the why and wherefore of what he did. He learned to make concrete, shovelling it over three times dry and three times wet. Then it came to bricks and mortar, and he learned how to make mortar and smooth it before use. He had to carry it in a bucket for, with only one hand, he could not manage a hod. For the bricks, he contrived a barrow into which he could load and wheel them to the pile at Coles' hand. My father learned to respect his 'foreman's' tantrums. He knew he must not keep him waiting, must keep the bricks clean and bring the mortar without lumps, for Coles would throw the dirty bricks in my father's direction, or splatter him with mortar as he swept a trowel towards him.

My father had to keep his own temper well in check, for he knew that any sign of rebellion on his part would leave him with an unfinished building and no bricklayer. Despite this, he must have shown his anxiety to get the building finished too clearly. One evening when my father urged that they should go on laying floorboards by the light of a lantern, he had a strike on his hands:

'You drive me all the time,' Coles said, low and quickly. 'It's not fair, you driving me to death. You ought to pay me my right money. You're saving yourself money all right, paying me ninepence an hour instead of one and threepence'.

He hurriedly collected his tools in a little sack, flung it over the handlebars of his bicycle and rode off. He didn't turn up next day. My father had to go and see him in his cottage and offer him a shilling an hour before he would resume work. But the building was finished by April, a month before the new baby's arrival. Few would have imagined that a man paralysed in the right arm and right leg could, even with such erratic skilled help, have built a shed let alone a substantial addition to a very old house. Moreover, as the years went by, the addition blended so completely into it that there was little sign that the original had been altered.

Some eight years after the extension to The Rosery was built, Mr Punnett decided to build an imposing house for himself. The Lodge had small rooms and a damp cellar. The front rooms faced North and were cold except for Mrs Punnett's den, where a fire always blazed brightly for the benefit of the parrot and brother William. The dogs lay on the hearthrug, drying out damp fur and muddy paws.

Mr Punnett built their new house, Applegarth, a handsome large brick house, opposite the Pines, using oak for all the doors and every floor board. Mrs Punnett, the parrot and the dogs moved into the new house; but she was not happy, and my mother often found her in tears. One day she opened a letter at breakfast and found a separation order. Mr Punnett no longer wanted her.

She moved to Woking with Christine, the maid who was devoted to her, the parrot and the dogs. But she had to work as a gardener to keep them all, and, after Christine's early death, became a recluse, no longer answering my mother's letters.

9 – THE CHRISTENING

Nurse Cannon – the Gills – Selina Storr saves the day –
Nannie Read takes over – 'Baby's Day' – a nose out of joint.

My mother wanted the new baby to be born at home. She knew
that my father would not want to stay in London at Ashburn
Place, more especially because the baby was due in May. He
would not want to leave The Rosery when the spring flowers
would still be in bloom, the birds singing their welcome to
summer and the kitchen garden, over which he had laboured so
lovingly, having to be hoed. A nursing home in Tunbridge Wells
had been suggested, but my mother could not bear the thought
that he would have to travel on the buses which had just started
to run to Tunbridge Wells. She knew she would suffer fears
that he had fallen over or fallen off the step of the bus or
been run over. In short, she could nor bear him out of her sight.
Therefore she must stay at home so that she always knew where
he was.

My mother's parents, the Munts, offered to pay for a monthly
nurse. A small, competent woman arrived, called Nurse
Cannon. She leaned her elbows on the table at teatime, which I
had been told was not good manners. After the new baby had
arrived, and was a girl, she remarked to me, 'Now your nose will
be out of joint'. A little later I looked anxiously at my face in the
long mirror on the wall at the end of the landing and, observing
that my nose was not crooked, I decided that Nurse Cannon had
been guilty not only of bad manners, but of telling lies.

Denis and I and Nannie had left The Rosery a few days before
the baby was born and were staying with Mr and Mrs Gill at
Boughton Colemers, opposite the church. They had come to live
in Matfield with their two teenage daughters soon after the war.
Mr Murton Gill was a Director of a London firm of accountants.
He was taken to Tunbridge Wells station every day by his
chauffeur, Wilson, who lived in the cottage at the big white gates

of the house. Wilson had been in the regular army and had luxuriant waxed moustaches.

The Gills had become very friendly with my parents. My mother had been one of their first callers. Louise, the youngest girl, told my mother:

'Deborah and I were looking out of the landing window, Eileen, when we saw you walking up the drive. We couldn't believe that someone so young and smart lived in Matfield!'

Mrs Gill and my mother became confidantes and it was proposed, and accepted gratefully, that Nannie and the children should stay at Boughton Colemers for a week or two, thus making room for Nurse Cannon and the nursery vacant for the infant. Probably my mother feared a repetition of the agonised screaming that had preceded Denis' birth would terrify the children. The walls of The Rosery were not soundproof. My father was nervous of the use of chloroform by a general practitioner but he had regretted he had not insisted on its use at Denis' birth. This time it would be used, he promised her.

On Sunday, 6 May, Anne, called 'Baby' for several years, was born. At Boughton Colemers, I was given a little wicker basket and told to pick flowers for my mother and the new sister. The house had a private wood and the primroses were thick, their yellow beauty shining on the green banks and in the sunny glades beneath the trees. There were clumps of wood violets, the tiny purple flowers almost hidden by the green leaves.

Nannie was grumpy. She loved tiny babies and was resentful that Nurse Cannon was installed in her nursery.

I was taken by my father into the bedroom looking out over the pear tree where my mother lay in bed, the treasure cot, newly refurbished in white, sprigged muslin by Nannie, beside her. I caught a glimpse of a tiny head, hardly bigger than Marie, my favourite doll.

Shortly after we returned to The Rosery, my parents went away for a month to an island on the Norfolk Broads, the home of an ornithologist, Miss Turner, whom my father greatly admired and who encouraged him to study and write about birds. She was elderly at this time but her friendship with my father had started when he was at Cambridge where she lived when not in Norfolk.

A sepia-coloured photograph shows my mother sitting in a wicker chair outside the wooden thatched hut that was their bedroom on this island. She was feeding the baby and it flourished but, so she told me, her mother was furious with my father for selfishly exposing her to the risks of such an unorthodox holiday.

On their return to Matfield, Baby was christened at Matfield Church. Her long, white, embroidered lawn robe, which had been my father's christening robe, was draped over Mrs Gill's arm. She was to be the godmother and held the baby. I was thinking more about my new white kid shoes than the importance of the occasion. Indeed, I was jealous of the attention Nannie now gave to Baby and resented her smoothing out the folds of the christening robe. I heard my father talking anxiously to the vicar. It seemed there was no water for the ceremony. I did not understand why water was necessary but Miss Selina Storr came hurrying up the path to the church porch with a brass jug. Everyone began to smile and I followed Nannie into church.

I was surprised that the christening took place at the back of the church, instead of the front where Mr Tomlinson always stood on Sundays. Now I knew what the big stone bath that stood beside our pew was for. I had seen Miss Selina pour the water from her jug into the bath, and now Mr Tomlinson held the baby and splashed some water on her face. I heard him say 'Anne Eileen' and understood that was to be Baby's name.

Everyone left the church and Mrs Gill, who now held Baby again, handed her to Nannie. Nannie, who was very good-tempered now that Nurse Cannon had left The Rosery, laid the baby in the big pram and arranged the covers as if for a picture. The crocheted pillowcase and pram cover, I knew she had made herself, for I had seen her busy with them in the nursery.

Nannie wheeled the pram proudly through the lychgate of the church and the short distance down the road to The Rosery. I held the handle on one side, quite pleased to be part of the centre of attention. I hoped that people noticed the beautiful tiny rose-buds encircling the crown of my straw hat. I asked Nannie if she thought they had. I felt disappointed when she replied, quite sternly, that it was 'Baby's day'.

In the weeks that followed, every day seemed to be 'Baby's day,' for Nannie was so busy with her new charge that she had little time for telling stories, which she was much better at than reading them. Nannie hummed softly to herself as she moved the flat iron (heated on the hob of the nursery fire) in and out of the tucks and frills on the long dresses which babies wore until they were six months old (when they, the babies, were said to be 'shortened').

My father would not have wished for another son, as he did when Anne and I were born, had he not been confident that there would never be another war. He thought that the fearful casualties of 1914 to 1918, such as had never been experienced before in any war, would deter future generations, in all countries, from military adventure. He also believed that the Christian message of love could at last be understood.

Dog Violets

10 – CHILDHOOD

*Nannie and Eileen – Christmas, 1923 – bus sacrificed –
William Willett of Sloane Square – syrup of figs – 'dying
together' – Gerald – the marmet pram – the broken glass-
house pane.*

My mother's early cosseted life as well as her temperament had
not conditioned her to be either a careful housekeeper or to
enjoy the routine of looking after young children. She performed
household tasks quickly but in a slapdash, hurried way as if she
were thinking of more urgent matters. This temperament of
course was the absolute antithesis of her mother-in-law's. It was
no wonder they didn't get on. The lists of household routine
drawn up by Grannie Willett soon vanished, if indeed they were
ever used.

My father was certainly not a tidy man, perhaps because, both
at University and in his home, servants had always tidied up for
him. Yet in the early years of their marriage he failed to
recognise that my mother's kindly, tolerant nature, her constant
loving desire to please and serve him, was the reverse side
of the coin that left her indifferent to the mud he always
brought into the house on his boots, the drawers and cupboards
that would never shut because of the muddle in them, and her
inability to 'train' the maids because she didn't think it
mattered.

Nannie gave a stability to our early childhood by adherence to
routine and an understanding of the needs of small children. She
was stickler for neatness and a marvellous needlewoman. She
made some of my dresses and many for the baby. My hair was
straight; she tied it up in rags at bedtime so that it was a mop of
curls in the morning. My father, who didn't get on with her,
stopped this hairdressing – a relief to me because I didn't enjoy
standing still while Nannie did up my hair at night and pulled out
the tangles in the morning.

65

I loved her more than I did my mother, who was totally preoccupied in watching and waiting on my father.

In my early childhood, or late babyhood, I did not see much of my mother. Meals were taken in the nursery with Nannie. I was with Nannie most of the day and at nights. At this stage of my life, I do not think my mother was much interested in me, although of course I was not neglected. Still, I perceived, with the accurate insight of a young child, that Denis was preferred; and when Anne arrived, perhaps because she knew this would be her last baby, she was drawn to her and made much of her. Yet my reliance on Nannie may have stood between us, for when Nannie left at the time I was nearly nine, I felt the strength of my mother's love and returned it.

The first Christmas after Anne was born, 1923, Nannie organised a Christmas tree. Denis and I were not allowed in the day nursery on Christmas Eve. We had our tea in front of the fire in the night nursery. My mother and father had moved into the new bedroom he had built, and we now slept with Nannie in the room looking out to the pear tree. Baby's cot was in the day nursery.

On Christmas morning Nannie flung open the door of the nursery: there was the tree, so large that it seemed to fill the room. It sparkled with gold and silver bells and at the top was a fairy doll. The branches bore lighted candles. Underneath was a pile of presents.

Best of all the presents was a model of a London bus, big enough for me to sit on the top deck which, of course, had no roof. It was a lovely thing.

I can't remember how long we had it, but one day it was given away. We had a teatime visit from a lady who had been a parlour maid in my father's old home. She came with her husband and her little girl. I remember my father seeking me out in the day nursery and explaining that the little visitor had hardly any toys and had taken a strong fancy to our bus. 'I feel sure you would like to be a kind little girl and give her something she wants so much,' he said quickly, as if fearful I would refuse. I always wanted to please my father, and was conscious that I didn't often achieve this aim. So of course I nodded my agreement, and the bus went. It was given to us by my father's aunt, Great Aunt Rebecca, who lived in Hove. Great Aunt Bec, who lived to be ninety but always seemed to me to be that age, was very kind to us. As long as she lived gave us a four-shilling piece or a five-shilling piece for Christmas. I often regretted that round about February I was driven by financial necessity to cash my big silver piece.

Great Aunt Bec was the widow of my father's Uncle Everard. My grandfather, Thomas, was his youngest brother. William, the eldest, inherited the family building business which had been founded by my great grandfather, also William Willett. My grandmother Willett told many stories of her father-in-law (who had once thrown the gravy tureen at a maid). In his younger days he had liked drinking, smoking, swearing and, as my grandmother put it, had liked the company of flighty women. All was changed (except his sometimes violent temper) after he had a 'vision', the details of which were unclear but after which he became excessively religious. When my grandmother was newly married and stayed with her parents-in-law, probably around 1885, she said it was irksome to see letters brought in by the Sunday post and not to be allowed to open them until Monday.

William Willett, the elder, had a rule book for his workmen which was strongly influenced by his religious principles. A man would be dismissed instantly if he was discovered drinking or smoking on a site. But although strict he was careful of his employees' welfare. The men were allowed to work only in daylight; their hours averaged 51 in summer and 47 in winter. Safety rules were rigidly enforced: no man must be asked to work in a dangerous position. Everyone had to pay into an Accident and Sickness Fund.

He was a good employer, too, to his firm's horses. They could get 'depressed ', he said, if they were left standing about in rain or a strong east wind, and, if the roads were muddy, their loads should be reduced from 600 to 500 bricks.

Great-grandfather was an inspired businessman and founded a firm which built many houses in Brighton, Hove and London. 'Willett-built' became synonymous for good standards, and he became very prosperous. The firm moved to Sloane Square in London.

On his death, his eldest son, William the younger, took over and was equally successful.

In the time the firm developed an estate agency arm which is now (1984) independent. The building operations became part of the Trafalgar House organisation in 1972.

Everard, the second son was a solicitor like my grandfather, Thomas. However, unlike Thomas, he developed a thriving practice. Great Aunt Bec had a big house in Cromwell Road, Hove. I stayed with her once for a few days and much enjoyed blowing down the speaking tubes, the method of communicating with the maids in the basement. At lunch, there would be a loud creaking and a trolley with food would come up through the floor from the basement kitchen. Great Aunt was probably wealthier than my grandparents, Thomas and Susie, but lived far less ostentatiously. She had two sons, both older than their first cousin, my father. The younger son, Tom, was 'delicate': this was a delicate disguise for his epileptic fits and, although he was married and lived almost next door to his mother, had no children. Everard, the older son, was also married and a successful solicitor. He also had no children. It was not known till much later that he was a homosexual. In the family no-one save his unfortunate wife had the secret. She was a very old lady, a widow for many years, before she told anyone how unhappy the marriage had been.

Nannie was fond of telling us about the children she looked after before she came to us. One of them was the child of a doctor. Kenneth was a sickly baby, a poor little thing, said Nannie and before her arrival looked as if he might die. 'I put him on Nestlé's milk,' related Nannie triumphantly.' and he began to thrive.' Nannie was a staunch believer in Nestlé's concentrated milk, and usually had a tin in her cupboard in the nursery. I loved its sweet taste. Nannie would sometimes give me a spoonful of it to make up for a dose of syrup of figs. This deadly concoction was also on standby in the nursery cupboard. I dreaded it, starting to retch as it was uncorked. When I could read the inscription 'Children love it' I used to wonder where the

68

makers had managed to find such children. I hated all medicines and later, at school, when I had to go to matron's room after lunch for a tablespoon of cod liver oil and malt, I used to clench the spoon in my teeth and rush out to the bathroom to wash it for matron, an operation that enabled me to swill most of the treacly substance down the sink.

The Rosery still had dark blinds, a legacy from the War and zeppelin raids. Nannie liked to relate her experiences of one such raid. 'The whole family, maids and all, gathered in the dining room,' she said. I was impressed at this display of solidarity, but puzzled. 'Why did you do that, Nannie?' I asked. 'To die together!' she replied, as if it were the most ordinary thing in the world. For a moment I was transported to that far-off dining room in some grand London house. I seemed to hear a terrific bang. Nannie and all the people vanished as the house fell down, like a pack of cards in *Alice in Wonderland*, my favourite book at the time. The sight of Nannie prosaically squeezing toothpaste onto my brush brought me back to the bathroom at The Rosery.

For my fifth birthday Nannie gave me Gerald, a large china baby doll with dark hair and blue eyes, which opened and shut. It must have cost her all the money she earned in a month. She had made all the clothes herself: the lawn petticoat and flannel petticoat were edged in crocheted lace. The dress had rows and rows of inset lace threaded with blue ribbon.

It was my most treasured possession. At night, as I lay in bed, I imagined that the house was on fire and I escaped through the window with Gerald.

Nannie was happiest with babies and small children who enjoyed her large repertoire of nursery rhymes. The nursery was a cosy, safe world. Yet, although I continued to find security in Nannie's care, I was growing out of it. I was still jealous of Anne because she took up so much of Nannie's time, and I was often sent out into the garden to play by myself.

I had a big doll's pram, a replica of a 'marmet' which Nannie (as well as the Royal Family) considered the only acceptable make of pram. My pram had been given to me by Mrs Plummer, who lived at Becketts Grove, beyond the Grange School. Major

Plummer was a genial, black-haired man with a clipped moustache. He developed pneumonia when he was less than fifty years old and, despite the attention of the Brenchley doctor, supplemented by the advice of a specialist who drove down from London — at a guinea a mile — Major Plummer died. Antibiotics would have saved him, but they had not yet been discovered. Mrs Plummer sold Becketts Grove and moved to London with her two daughters. Before she left, she gave The Rosery three useful presents: a big wooden hut, a long teak seat used every Summer for tea on the front lawn, and my doll's pram.

Nannie was very particular that I should be wrapped up warmly when I went out into the garden. Usually this meant a woolly hat, a big scarf crossed over my chest and tied at the back, and gaiters. These were brown leather. They were anchored by straps under the shoes. Rows of boot buttons went up the legs. Each had to be fastened with a button hook.

I took equal care with Gerald, and Nannie always helped me wrap him up in the pram. I was quite happy as I trundled the pram round the garden paths. Once I disobeyed the instruction 'not to sit down'. I sat on my father's winter garden frame, under which he was growing marrows and spring vegetables. I broke a pane in the glass, which seemed to me a dreadful calamity. I had been told by my mother never to upset him, and now I had done it. I left Gerald in his pram and stood close to his study window. I could see him inside working at his desk. Suddenly he looked up, feeling that he was being watched and saw my tearful face. In a minute, I was inside, held against his knee as I sobbed out my confession. He wiped away my tears and promised me I should help him put a new pane in next day. He could be loving as well as stern.

11 – HOME EDUCATION

Parental impatience – escape into Victorian stories – my father's companion – Angelina the ferret.

I loved the flowers. In March the big double daffodils in the garden entranced me, then the primroses, the violets under the hedges, the bluebells in the little wood. Then the roses. There was a big pink cabbage rose bush, near the old cesspool (we were not on main drainage), where I always lingered, pressing my face against its sweet smelling petals. Every day in June I waited for the blooming of the Albrecht Barbier, the white rose on the front lawn. I liked it best in bud when the colour was creamy yellow.

Denis was sent to board at a boys' preparatory school in the village at the age of six, but my father decided to teach me himself to save private school fees in Tunbridge Wells. The village school was of course not considered. Indeed, for some years my brother and I were the only children who were not, as they were euphemistically called, 'village children'.

It was fortunate that I was fond of reading. My father, whose lessons I did not enjoy, taught me to read by the time I was six. Lessons began every morning at nine o'clock. My father started with a prayer while we both kneeled on the carpet. His intentions were so good, that he would be patient and gentle with me. However before the hour was over, he would have become enraged with my early childish incomprehension. The more he shouted his impatience the more mistakes I made. On one occasion he banged my head not too gently on the table. I was always so anxious to please him that this incident grieved me more because I had failed than because I was hurt. But he never forgot his occasional bursts of intemperance. Many times as the years passed I had to reassure him that I had forgiven him.

I soon learned to do well in a dream world peopled mostly by characters from the Victorian writer Mrs Molesworth's stories for young children. Nevertheless I was very excited to hear my mother speak of a little girl who was coming to live at the Grove. For days I peered through the hedge that divided the gardens and hoped that the child would like my dolls, Marie and Gerald, and perhaps show me hers. Alas, I discovered that I could not meet her: she was the housekeeper's daughter. My mother told me this. She had no strong feelings about class herself, but she was expressing opinions shared by most people at the time.

My father was determined to do with one hand and a paralysed leg what he had achieved as a strong and able-bodied man. He played tennis and fell over. He climbed ladders and fell off. He swam a very short distance. He walked longer and further than most people did, even then.

Because I was a strong child, my brother was at school, and my sister still a baby, I had to become his constant companion. Afraid that he might fall over and lie lost in the many woods that surrounded the village I had to appear eager to accompany him on these long walks, for he was too proud to accept reluctance. It was not long before I acquired an anxiety complex, weighed down by my responsibility, at the age of six. At night my legs would ache so that I would sometimes cry with the pain. It was said that these were 'growing pains'.

The Rosery had gradually deteriorated from Grandmother's masterpiece of 1916. The white paint on the skirting boards had chipped, the mahogany furniture was scratched, one armchair in the drawing room developed a broken leg, never repaired. It had to be moved out of the way of visitors but it could be used if one remembered to sit on it carefully. One of the banister rails came out of the wall plaster and was never mended. Indeed, as a general rule anything that broke remained so. The only exception was the broken floorboard in the kitchen, over which my father nailed a short board liable to trip anyone up who didn't know it was there. The rats and mice, which had been banished when my parents first took over The Rosery, returned and could be heard at night under the floorboards. I remember one morning waking to find my Aunt Evelyn, who had been staying with us (she was my mother's half-sister) asleep beside me. On waking she explained that she had been woken up by a mouse pattering across the floor and was so terrified she had taken refuge with me.

I was as frightened of rats and mice as she was. One of the reasons I gave up climbing into the outhouse loft was that I saw a rat sitting on the trunk. They were also in the outhouse where the grain to feed the chickens was kept. As I had once seen a rat jump out of the grain bin, I always took care to bang the outhouse door several times before entering, knowing that any rats would have disappeared when I got in.

My father decided that something must be done about the rats. He purchased a ferret which we called Angelina. He said Angelina could be my pet and I should have the job of feeding her. But Angelina proved to be an expert at biting the hand that fed her. As I opened her cage to insert her saucer of food or water, she would lunge forward and often succeed in giving my fingers a sharp nip. My 'pet' became an object of fear, although I never dared to tell my father, who of all things abhorred cowardice. What magicial relief it was when I approached the cage one morning to find Angelina had vanished, presumably through a hole she had bitten in the floor. Happily, she was never found.

Short-eared Owl

12 – CHURCHWARDEN

The Vicar – the Misses Storr show their hand – the invitation accepted – high and low church – sherry after church – disarmament – seat near the font – Curly Fuller.

One day the vicar knocked at the front door and asked for my father, who was in the garden planting out lettuces. Clara called him in and brought in the tea: bread and butter and cherry cake on the silver tray donated by grandmother Willett.

'Well, Mr Willett, I am wondering whether I might ask you to be my churchwarden at the Easter vestry meeting,' Mr Tomlinson said in a serious voice: 'Mr Perkin is giving up after some years of splendid service. I don't want to press you for an answer today, but will you consider it?'

Although my father was pleased and anxious to accept a position he felt would make use of his abilities in active Christianity as well as giving him standing in the village, he felt that to agree immediately would disappoint the vicar, who obviously expected him to pray for God's guidance over the next few days. So he answered:

'Of course, I would like time to consider whether I am fitted for such responsibility, but is there no older man you would perhaps prefer?'

'In confidence,' said the vicar, 'I have had some trouble. When Mr Perkin said he would have to resign, Mr Pugh, the other churchwarden, who is a cousin to the Misses Storr, went off and told Mr Porter at the Post Office that he was to be warden in his place. I couldn't allow that, because not only is Porter a former chapel member; he is not an educated man with whom I could talk things over with ease. And, in any case, the vicar is by custom allowed to choose his own churchwarden. Mine is a difficult position,' he went on, warmed by my father's sympathetic listening. 'They drove the last incumbent out.'

'Who did?' said my father, bewildered.

'The Storrs. They make it difficult for me. Their father was the first vicar here. When he retired he built his house opposite the vicarage. He and his wife and the daughters come into the vicarage all the time and tell me what I ought or ought not to do. And of course the nephew being churchwarden makes it doubly difficult for me'.

This more than confirmed the local gossip of the domination by the Storr families of everything that happened in the village. They could, and often did, obtain the dismissal of anyone who offended against their puritanical code of morals.

My father was more than ever anxious to accept the wardenship so that he could back the vicar against such feudal tyranny. When my mother returned from her afternoon tea party, she was at first incredulous:

'I can't imagine you as a churchwarden, Wilfred,' she said, no doubt mindful of the venerable gentlemen who had performed the function in her family's church in London.

'I shall make a very good one,' he replied, confidently. 'But it's a serious undertaking, and I shall have to think about it.'

At the end of the week, he called on the vicar and accepted the office. He attended the Easter services accompanied by my mother, proud to be the wife of the new churchwarden and happy because of his pleasure.

Mr Pugh and my father made the collection together. As the vicar raised the offertory salver in a symbolic gesture to God, my father stood reverently to attention. He was filled with confusion when, glancing sideways, he saw that Mr Pugh had already resumed his seat in the first pew.

When my father questioned the vicar in the vestry as to whether Mr Pugh had not shown lack of reverence in not waiting while the offerings were dedicated, the vicar replied:

'I know Mr Pugh does not make it easy, but he is always wary of what he regards as high church practices.'

'I'll go and see him and explain it's the usual way in most churches and in no way high church,' confidently replied my father.

'Oh no, you mustn't do that,' said the vicar hastily. 'We must leave it for the present.'

75

My father had become an enthusiastic supporter of high church principles and had many talks with the vicar who, although agreeing, did not want to be open about it:

'I must be careful not to divide the parish into two camps,' he said. 'It would make it very difficult for me.'

My father's philosophic talks with the vicar, in which he was forever vainly urging more activity in making the villagers aware of the church's role in disarmament and brotherhood between nations, usually took place in the hour after congregation had dispersed and after the money had been counted in the vestry. Mr Pugh had of course departed. I believe the vicar and my father conversed over two glasses of sherry. The glasses and the sherry, unknown to the Storrs, were kept in the vicar's locker.

My mother seldom attended church after the first occasion when my father officiated as vicar's warden. But she didn't like him going alone. Soon after I was five, Nannie dressed me in my best clothes and hat and I accompanied him to Sunday morning service. This practice continued for several years, and I got used to waiting for him in the churchyard after the congregation had departed. Fearful of being caught sitting on the recumbent stones, I usually sat in the church porch, which was dark and gloomy or wandered between the grave stones. This was more interesting when I was able to read the inscriptions and, although there was nothing to equal Ebenezer's Zippor Buggs, I often stood by the graves of small children wondering why they had died so young.

Our family pew was at the back of the church, next to the door. I liked this arrangement because I could see the people sitting in front without them seeing me looking at them rather than following the service. Sometimes my father allowed me to stand on the seat when I was still too small to look over the rail of the pew. The Widow Storr sat with her daughters and nieces in one of the centre front pews. The boys of the Grange Preparatory School, where Denis was a boarder, sat in a row of pews on the right hand aisle of the church. They wore grey flannel suits with short trousers and a striped red and white tie. Their red caps in Winter and grey flannel hats in Summer lay on the seats beside them. Immediately before the sermon, there would be a tremendous shuffling of feet and they would file out, led by Miss Marjory Perkins, the Headmaster's sister.

When the church door opened, I caught a glimpse of the bright day outside and longed to follow them out of the dark church. The sermon was often very long and I thought about other things. My father always followed the sermon intently and glared at me if I fidgetted. It was a splendid moment when the vicar descended from his pulpit and collected his notes from the brass eagle lectern, presented by the Storrs.

The last hymn was always sung with noticeable spirit by the congregation, relieved that they would soon be setting out for home and Sunday lunch. Curly Fuller, so called because of the curls, now grey and thinning, which adorned his head, was the leading singer. Vainly did the ladies of the choir strive to raise their voices above his. No matter what the tune, Curly sang every word in a loud monotone, his unmistakable voice cracking in a way I have never heard before or since. He never missed a service because he had only to cross the road from his tumbledown cottage, with a well in the garden, in Bramble Reed Lane where he lived alone.

House Sparrow

77

13 — IN DEBT

Hairdressing — dog breeding — another threat to the allowance — debts paid, with a warning.

My mother's step-father died a year or two after the birth of my sister. This event caused a financial crisis. Nannie's wages had been paid by my grandmother. She and grandfather had often given Eileen presents of money which were helpful in meeting the bills of an expanding family. When grandfather died, he was found not to be a rich man. And he had had eight children, including my mother and Auntie Vi.

Auntie Vi, my mother's sister, was married to a wealthy solicitor, and so received no bequest under her step-father's will. The income on the letting of Ashburn Place was to be my grandmother's for life and then to be divided between his youngest daughter, Evelyn, and my mother, in the proportion of two-thirds to one-third, a recognition of the superior claim of a daughter over a step-daughter. But he left my mother the family silver engraved with the Munt crest, a bleeding head dripping blood.

Money difficulties at The Rosery did not diminish. There were two living-in maids, Nannie and a gardener. The gardener's wages were paid by grandmother Willett, but Nannie and the living-in maids were another matter. My father was anxious to give Nannie notice. He had never got on with her, thinking her management of small children old-fashioned and secretly, I believe, jealous of the affection I had for her. My mother realised that Nannie freed her to look after my father, and felt she could not do without her. The living-in maids, Clara and Hetty, were found other situations. Mrs Cheeseman, who lived in one of the row of cottages on the way to the village, was engaged to come and 'do' in the mornings. Nannie was not pleased that she had to make tea and supper for the children and, moreover, that the kitchen range often went out and was difficult to re-light so that there was no hot water for baths. I was miserable, as over the next year or two friction grew between Nannie and my father. I often heard angry voices as they argued with each other.

A friend of my mother must have suggested to her that she could earn money by training as a hairdesser. It would have been hard to imagine anyone less suited for the careful, orderly work required, yet my mother paid a premium to a London establishment and commenced her training. It cannot have lasted more than few weeks, for she found it insupportable to leave my father for hours every day. A few relics of this strange episode remained at The Rosery for years. A couple of school exercise books scrawled with 'lecture notes' were nearly indecipherable, although I could usually read my mother's odd handwriting. There were also two white overalls which were used in the next 'money-making' venture, dog breeding. Finally a pair of curling tongs, used occasionally to curl up my straight hair for parties. The tongs were heated until almost red-hot on the kitchen range and then my mother anxiously tried them out on a piece of newspaper. When the newspaper stopped bursting into flames, she applied them to my hair.

Some time after, my mother bought four pekinese dogs, and commenced her breeding kennels. Mrs Plummer's gift, the large wooden shed with a floor, was erected near the back door, and my father made a run round it with chicken wire and a paling gate.

My mother took one of the dogs to a pekinese show in London. Although he did not win a prize, she made the acquaintance of Miss Marjorie and Miss Cynthia Ashton Cross, then the doyennes of the pekinese world. Their kennels were renowned for producing dogs with placid temperaments with which the pekinese breed was not universally blessed. From the Misses Ashton Cross, she bought a bitch called Dinah who produced several litters. Some of these puppies were sold at a profit. But a beautiful black puppy, Jack, who might have been sold to Miss Ashton Cross for a large sum, moved into the house and became the family pet, surviving until the outbreak of the Second World War.

At one time there were ten dogs living in the hut. It was my task to let them out of their run once a day and shepherd them onto the tennis court for exercise. Invariably I lost control of the 'team' as they headed straight past the tennis court at a gallop with me in hot pursuit. Usually I was able to round them up in the vegetable garden, but on one occasion they tore through a hole in the fence into the next garden, belonging to The Grove, the large Victorian house next to The Rosery. At the time its inhabitants were two ladies called Miss Barnes and Miss Macfarlane. In those far off times no-one thought it was anything other than convenience and companionship that led two ladies to share a house. In retrospect I remember that Miss Macfarlane had very short hair (an 'eton crop' as it was called) and a mannish style of dressing. I remember I found her terrifying, never more so than when she suddenly materialised to watch me, with torn clothes and a scratched face, trying to chase the dogs back through the hedge into The Rosery garden.

Pekinese breeding lasted little more than a year. A litter of dead puppies and another of puppies with large noses which had to be given away, warned that the breeding venture was not making money. All the dogs except Jack and one of the large-nosed puppies called Blackie were found good homes. The hut was removed to the far end of the garden, where it became my father's outdoor study and writing room. Over the door he placed a plaque, 'Whoever shall come, be he friend, or foe, beggar or thief, let him be welcomed with kindness'.

He adopted a regular routine of writing all the morning. There were bird articles, but more seriously a war novel he had begun, encouraged by his friend, Henry Williamson, the author of *Tarka the Otter* and *Salar the Salmon*, who had been in his battalion at Ploegsteert Wood. In the afternoon, my father planted vegetables and worked on horticultural theories for crossing strains of flowers and fruit. He grew pumpkins, one so large that we took it to the harvest festival in the church on a wheelbarrow.

Then, of course, he did the church accounts with such unusual efficiency for a churchwarden that the rural dean wrote to the vicar complimenting him on his churchwarden's skill, not only with the church books, but also for his ability in suggesting money-raising schemes for new churches.

My father's own accounts still failed to balance. He wrote to his father asking if he could pay off £50 in bills owing and increase the allowance. Grandfather Willett had inherited an income of £3,000 a year, then a huge sum, from his father; so this did not seem an unreasonable request. However when my father called at The Homestead answering a curt message that he should do so, he found a storm brewing. Debt was abhorrent to them. Wilfred must cut his coat according his cloth.

After some minutes of this lecture, my father grew angry. He accused his mother of buying expensive clothes and taking extravagant holidays while he and his family had to manage on much less than a quarter of his parents' income.

My grandfather replied sharply: if Wilfred ever again criticised his mother, he would stop the allowance. Considering what sacrifices she had always made for him, it was most ungrateful. An apology should be made immediately. Over the next day or two they would discuss what could be done about the deplorable situation.

My grandmother added that, if Eileen were a better manager, they could live very comfortably at The Rosery. When my father defended her, she said:

'You must allow your mother to know best.' Grandfather chipped in:

'I am convinced you would not have insulted your mother unless at Eileen's instigation'.

My father was now frightened that if more was said they were quite capable of having nothing more to do with him and his family. So, muttering an apology, he kissed his mother dutifully and left.

A few days later he had a note from grandfather saying that he would pay the outstanding bills direct if they were sent to him, but that if ever Wilfred got into debt again the allowance would be stopped immediately.

14 – THE BLINDS PULLED DOWN

Tragedy and crisis – A doctor's error? – Sisterly estrangement –
Queen Alexandra.

Early one afternoon in 1925, we had just finished lunch in the
nursery at The Rosery when Nannie pulled the blinds down. I
followed her into the bedrooms and she was pulling the curtains
together.

'Why are you doing that, Nannie,' I asked 'It's not night yet.'

'It's Mrs Gill's funeral' she replied, shortly. Peeping
underneath the blind, I saw my mother and father walking down
the path, dressed in black. He was carrying his top hat, which
was always kept in the cupboard under the stairs and which I had
trod on a few weeks before when playing hide-and-seek.

Mrs Gill was buried in Matfield churchyard, her grave as near
to her former home, Boughton Colemers, as it could have been.
But the Gills had left Matfield six months before and Boughton
Colemers was now occupied by Mr and Mrs Burman and two
daughters, Vera and Dolly.

I knew that Mrs Gill had been very ill. But it was not until
some years afterwards that I heard how my mother had been
involved in the sad circumstances of her death.

Mrs Gill was just over fifty years of age when it was found that
she had an inoperable tumour on the brain. Mr Gill was
distraught, seeking comfort from my parents, for his daughters
were aged seventeen and eighteen and preoccupied with many
young men who flocked around them. Louise and Deborah were
beautiful. When I was very small I thought Louise looked like
a fairy princess. They were engaged, the younger to her cousin,
the son of Mrs Gill's sister. He was, or wanted to be, a farmer,
and Mr Gill had already decided to buy a big estate with an
Elizabethan house, Goddards Green, at Cranbrook. The whole
family were to move there, with arrangements for a separate
apartment for the young couple when they were married.

The plans were far advanced, and despite Mrs Gill's illness they went ahead. Mrs Gill was looked after devotedly by the family's housekeeper, Elizabeth, who had been with them many years. The house was a sad one and my mother visited it frequently, taking the bus to Cranbrook.

One afternoon, the telephone rang at The Rosery and my mother answered it. Mr Gill besought her to come at once: something terrible had happened. His ward, the orphaned daughter of a colleague, had given birth to a boy. She had complained of violent stomach pains and the doctor had been called. She did not know that she was pregnant. The doctor, who knew the family, had been shaken out of his professional calm when he discovered she was in labour. The girl, Cecily, was now in a state of shock. Mr Gill asked my mother to come and bring some clothes for the child. He had been wrapped up in a blanket and no-one in the house except Mrs Gill, who was too ill to be told, had any idea how to look after a newly-born infant. He had refused to let the doctor get a nurse because of the scandal.

Mr Gill said Wilson, the chauffeur, was already on his way to fetch her from The Rosery. Hastily bundling up some of Anne's baby clothes and shawls and her own night clothes, my mother was waiting when he arrived.

When she arrived at Goddards Green, Mr Gill met her at the door. He said that nobody had noticed any change in Cecily.

Indeed, my mother had seen her frequently and had never suspected that she might be pregnant. Mr Gill had had a stormy interview with the young man who was engaged to her. He admitted he loved her passionately but had no idea that there was a baby coming. Mr Gill, her guardian, now told him he was to leave the house without seeing Cecily until he had had time to think things over.

'What shall I do?' he said to my mother 'Evelyn [his wife] is dying. I can't think of anything else except her. Why didn't they think of her and me,' he added bitterly, 'before letting such a thing happen.' My mother tried to comfort him, but he was in despair. His ward had disgraced him and his wife would soon be dead.

When my mother saw Cecily, she looked like a child, with her fair plaits hanging over her shoulders. She cried that she couldn't understand how it happened. She didn't love her fiancé any more. She didn't want to see the baby.

My mother and Elizabeth dressed the baby and made a cradle for him out of a drawer. 'Elizabeth and I were both crying,' my mother told me years later. 'The baby was big and looked so sweet, poor little thing. He wasn't premature.'

My mother went to the bedroom Elizabeth had prepared for her and fell into a troubled sleep, thinking of the sorrows in the old house. She was awakened by a tap on the door:

'Miss Eileen! Miss Eileen! [so Elizabeth always called her.] Will you come? I've just been to look at the baby and he is lying so still and looks so white. I think he's dead.'

My mother sprang out of bed and soon confirmed Elizabeth's fears. The baby was dead. He had lived ten hours.

My mother said afterwards that she wondered if, in his surprise and distress, the doctor had not been skilful with the delivery and that the baby had received some internal injury at birth. Whatever it was, only she and Elizabeth shed tears as arrangements were hastily made for an inquest and private funeral.

My mother stayed for a day or two more, but could do little to comfort Mr Gill or ease his anger. 'If only Evelyn were well,' he frequently said, 'But now I have to decide everything.'

A month later Cecily married her fiancé and left Cranbrook. Mr Gill corresponded with her for some years and when my mother enquired, he said she was happy and had children.

But there were more troubles for Mr Gill at Goddards Green as well as his grief for his wife. His daughter, Louise, now 18, broke her engagement and wanted to marry her fiancé's brother who had returned from service in India. Mr Gill liked the elder brother and favoured the marriage. But Mrs Gill's sister was totally opposed and, despite Mrs Gill's grave illness, the sisters quarrelled bitterly. Mrs Gill never forgave her. On her death bed, which occurred within the year, she refused to see her sister. 'When she came to the side of her bed', Elizabeth told me 'Mrs Gill turned her head away and would not look at her.'

Soon after Mr Gill sold Goddards Green and moved first to

Eastbourne and then to Walmer with his two faithful retainers, Elizabeth and Beatrice, once the parlourmaid, now the cook. As I grew older I was often invited to spend a few days with them and enjoyed long walks along the sea front in winter and bathing in the summer. A framed text always stood on his dressing table: 'There is no death, there is but transition'. He survived his wife nearly thirty years until he reached 80.

Goddards Green was always supposed to be a haunted house. Nannie said she had heard that at midnight horses' hooves could be heard galloping up the drive. I think, though, that the sad happenings in that house in 1925 were haunting enough without fear of supernatural activity.

Later that year — it was winter — I was standing at the back door waiting for the milkman because I loved to see him open his churn, unhook one of his big measures and pour the lovely creamy milk into the jugs which Mrs Cheesman had left on the scullery table. I was surprised to see my mother and Louise Gill walk round the corner of the house dressed in black. They were wearing almost identical knee length dresses and hats like saucepans. I supposed they must be wearing black for Mrs Gill, but later Nannie told me that Queen Alexandra had died and people were wearing black 'out of respect for royalty'.

15 — GENERAL STRIKE

Crystal and cat's whisker — bridge — the Russians — holiday postponed — Uncle Lewis and the Daily Telegraph *— Susie's toughness — Winston Churchill's* British Gazette.

The unemployment figures were troubling my father. He now had a wireless and could listen to discussions. A teacher from the village school, a man with Labour sympathies with whom my father had had many friendly disagreements, had made himself a set with a crystal and cat's whisker and agreed to make one for The Rosery.

The preparations were watched with excitement by the whole family. An old tank, with an earth wire soldered on to it, was buried, a seven-strand copper wire was slung high between two trees, leads into the set arranged. By the end of the week the set was finished. Music and a man talking in London could be heard in the study at The Rosery.

Not long after this technical marvel, the General Strike began in 1926. There was little disturbance of Matfield's ways. The buses stopped running, but the twelve o'clock whistle or siren continued to be heard so that men on the farms would know the time to stop for lunch. Few wore watches. If they had them, they were pocket watches, kept for Sundays or special occasions.

Politics were not very real in Matfield. They were something to be read in the morning paper in the big houses. Nonetheless, the General Strike found its way into bridge table conversations. My mother and father now played regularly. Once a week they would dress in evening clothes and either go to other houses in Matfield to play, or the bridge table would be set up in the drawing room at The Rosery. I was always excited when I saw the preparations, although my father often got cross when try-ing to tie his evening bow tie with one hand. Sometimes he called me to hold the end of it but I was not a very successful helper and was glad to be let off so I could slip into the kitchen and help my mother put out the chocolate biscuit fingers. She always let me make the criss-cross pyramid. At 'half-time' at bridge parties the biscuits and tongue sandwiches were served, with coffee, and I liked to eat the pile of crusts as my mother carefully cut them off.

The nine-day General Strike in May 1926 co-incided with a bridge evening at The Rosery. Mr and Mrs Punnett were guests with Mr and Mrs Turner who had rented a house in Brenchley for the Summer. Mrs Punnett didn't play bridge so there were always two people 'sitting out'.

My father recollected the conversation in his later writings: He was playing bridge with Mr Punnett and Mr and Mrs Turner.

'It's all done by the Russians,' stated Mr Punnett, 'That there should be people who want to turn England Bolshevik: it's incredible!'

'The agitators are bribed with fabulous sums in gold stolen from the Russian banks,' claimed Mr Turner, with emphasis.

My father's contribution was:

'No decent working man wants to make England into the state Russia is in. Starvation always hits the working class. They'd start a bloody revolution tomorrow to get the things that don't belong to them in justice.'

'Surely, dear old England, with all her faults is too happy a place for anything like that,' put in a soothing Mrs Turner, for Mr Punnett was banging the bridge table to emphasise his point.

'Hadn't we better get on with the game if we are to finish before midnight?' intervened Mr Turner.

The only inconvenience my parents had to put up with was the postponement of a holiday in Norfolk. Grandmother Susie had offered to take them with her to a hotel in Yarmouth on the strength of a lucky coup on the Stock Exchange. She decided, however, that it was much too dangerous to risk her new car on the journey there.

'Bands of hooligans are stopping cars and throwing bricks through the windows,' she said, shaking her head, 'Lewis says its very serious. We're on the verge of a revolution. He is told a lot by the Government now that he is one of the managers of *The Daily Telegraph*.

Uncle Lewis was my father's youngest brother. He was less clever than my father and had not wanted to go to university. In the Black Watch Regiment during the War, he had escaped with only a minor wound and now, having obvious talents as an organiser, was earning a good salary as a circulation manager in Fleet Street.

'Lewis says we are safe as anywhere in Tunbridge Wells,' went on my grandmother, seriously. My mother said afterwards that grandmother would have been quite capable of dealing with a dozen hooligans. Although this was not meant to be praise, it was clear to me in later years that, although my father's idealism, his passion for causes, was inherited from the Willetts, his enormous physical courage had been bestowed upon him by his mother, Susie Seager. In the Battle of Britain in the Second World War I sat opposite her in her house in Tunbridge Wells, trembling with fear, as the house repeatedly shook with bomb blasts. She was reading with an outsize magnifying glass which she always used instead of spectacles. I observed that her hand was quite steady, holding the glass and moving it backwards and forwards over the book.

After the strike had been on a few days, Mr Punnett brought my father a copy of *The British Gazette* that Winston Churchill was running for the Government and which he had brought to London. Mr Punnett had daringly driven himself to London and back.

16 – SCHOOL

Magic lantern slides – a day too soon – General Ward and the Zulu Wars – independence and 'insubordination' – competition in class – paratyphoid fever.

Delights of my early childhood were the invitations to events at the Grange School. Every Christmas term there was a conjuror who had an audience most willing to believe that the tricks were a kind of magic. I longed to put up my hand when he asked for a helper but did not dare. Then there was an evening of magic lantern slides when we seemed to sit for a long time in darkness waiting for the slides to be sorted. Often one appeared upside down. These were occasions which I looked forward to for weeks. In Summer, the Grange sports day was eagerly awaited. I was always the first to appear at the starting line of the strangers' race, but I never won it.

When I was nearly seven I started school at the High School, Tunbridge Wells. The headmistress, Miss East, was later the distinguished headmistress of Blackheath High School. My mother took me on the first day. As I walked up Grove Hill with her to the big square High School at the top, I was pleased with my new white blouse and blue and black tie, gym slip and black velour hat with blue and black ribbon. I was not so pleased with my blue reefer coat, which had been given to me by one of my mother's friends. It had belonged to her daughter and was much too big, but Miss Childs had cut off a few inches from the hem and sewn up the pockets, which then appeared somewhere at thigh level. My fears that it looked slightly ridiculous were afterwards confirmed by another girl, who asked if it had come from a jumble sale. I denied this hotly, affirming that the sewn-up pockets were pleats.

My mother rang the bell at the front door of the school and after a few minutes it was opened by a tall, thin lady, obviously Miss East. She looked surprised.

'This is Marjorie,' said my mother, 'Marjorie Willett.'

'But school begins tomorrow,' said Miss East.

Then probably noting my crestfallen face she said kindly:

'Well as you're here, come in and I'll ask Marjorie some questions and set her a little exam so we can decide what form she is to be in.'

Despite starting school two years after my contemporaries I was put in Form II with girls of my own age.

My pleasure in school was all the more intense for having had no-one to share my lessons or play with. Also my work was praised and I found it not difficult to get high marks.

School ended for the day at one o'clock, except on Tuesdays when there was net ball in the afternoon. I could have had lunch on Tuesdays at school, but in order to save the expense my grandmother arranged that I should go to the house of friends of hers, General and Mrs Ward at No. 7 Calverley Park.

Calverley Park was a private road, on the left hand side of Grove Hill. The houses were designed by a famous architect called Decimus Burton. When I rang the bell at No. 7, a maid answered and took my coat and hat and showed me into the winter garden to await the arrival of Mrs Ward from her morning's shopping. The winter garden had many potted plants and four or five canaries in beautiful gilded cages. They sang very sweetly. Although I was usually hungry, I didn't mind waiting for the very good lunch shortly to be served in the gloomy dining room with swords and battle flags hanging on the walls. The General, a very old man who had fought in the Zulu War of 1879 and the Boer War of 1900-01, sat at the head of the long table, Mrs Ward at the foot, and I in the middle, half-way down.

In the hall was a big table on which, under glass, were all the General's medals. Mrs Ward was his second wife. She had a low voice and was very kind. I had the impression she was in awe of my grandmother Willett. However, after General Ward's death, I think she appreciated her friendship.

Grandmother had a Rover car and a chauffeur called Rout. She took Mrs Ward for drives in Ashdown Forest or in other beautiful country surrounding Tunbridge Wells. And, of course, she played bridge with her.

In The Rosery garden, 1922:
the thrush's egg.

The Rosery in 1916 '. . . in summer the front was covered with a mass of tiny white roses' (p. 27).

St Luke's Church and Matfield War Memorial (above) and the old Ebenezer and Chapel Row (below) 1919 (pp. 51 and 31).

Eileen with her first baby, 1918:
'. . . never happier than cradling him in her
arms' (p. 46).

Nannie Read, 1918: '. . . she no longer
expected ever to have children of her own'
(p. 47).

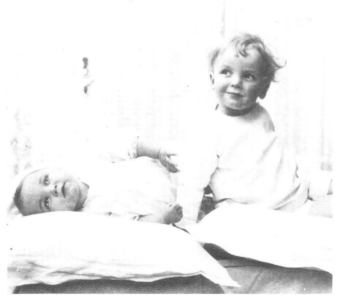

'. . . in the
rose-patterned
nursery above
the porch',
1920 (p. 53).

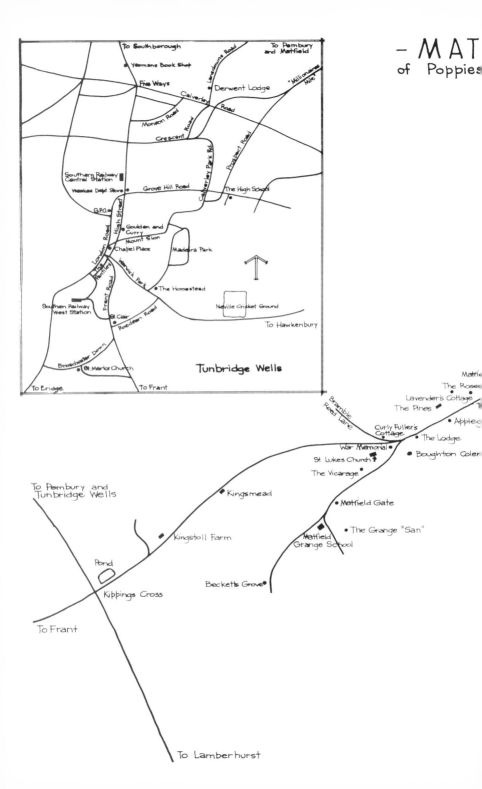

— MAT
of Poppies

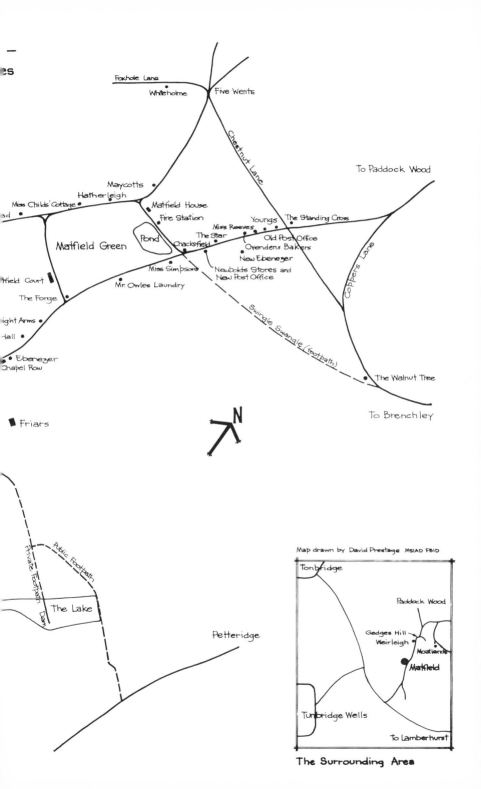

Foxhole Lane
Whiteholme
Five Wents
Chestnut Lane
To Paddock Wood

Maycotts
Hatherleigh
Miss Childs' Cottage
Matfield House
Fire Station
Youngs
The Standing Cross
Miss Reeves
The Star
Matfield Green
Pond
Chacksfield
Old Post Office
Ovendens Bakers
New Ebenezer
Coppers Lane
Miss Simpson
Newbolds Stores and
New Post Office
field Court
Mr. Owles Laundry
The Forge
Swingle Swangle (footpath)
ight Arms
Hall
Ebenezer
Chapel Row
The Walnut Tree
To Brenchley

Friars

N

Public Footpath
Private Footpath
Dam
The Lake
Petteridge

Map drawn by David Prestage MSIAD FBID
Tonbridge
Paddock Wood
Gedges Hill
Weirleigh
Moatlands
Matfield
Tunbridge Wells
To Lamberhurst

The Surrounding Area

'Miss Simpson lived in a white cottage (always called 'Miss Simpson's') next to Mr Owles' laundry' (p. 35).

'Deborah and I were looking out of the landing window [at Boughton Colemers], Eileen, when we saw you walking up the drive' (p. 62).

Newbold's Grocery Stores, Matfield, in the 1930's. The Newbold family: Mr and Mrs Newbold, Reg and Arthur Newbold (pp. 34 and 186).

A peep at the new baby sister: Nurse Cannon at The Rosery, May, 1923.

Anne.

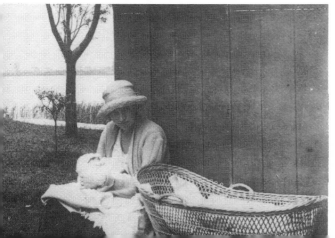

Eileen on Miss Turner's Island, Hickling Broad, June, 1923 (p. 62).

'Sadly, Miss Childs didn't own her cottage' (p. 98).

Matfield pond in foreground. 'Mallards still skimmed it, sometimes staying a few days' (p. 33). Matfield Green and distant view of the Forge.

Matfield House, on the Green, '. . . had a courtyard on the side with a clocktower on the outbuildings' (p. 33).

I reacted strongly to the companionship of girls of my own age for the first time in my life. From being an introspective, quiet, and serious child I became noisy, ready to break school rules if by doing so I could attract the admiration of the other girls, always ready to accept a 'dare'. At school, I felt I was responsible for nobody. No-one relied on me. I could do as I pleased. Not surprisingly my end of term reports began to refer to an 'insubordinate nature'. My father was much more interested in the comments on my work, and I believe he was as disappointed as I was when, in my third term, Miss East announced that marks were to be abolished, and there would be no form placings.

My spirit was competitive and I felt keen disappointment as the assembled girls rose — it was the end of the school year — to sing 'Forty Years On.' I rather liked the tune but thought the words were sad — forty years added to seven would make me 47! Miss East and some of the teachers would certainly be 'scattered asunder', in the words of the song, for they seemed to me already old. In forty years, they would perhaps be aged more than one hundred!

Miss East's 'experiment' in abolishing marks and placings lasted half a term. And a private school could easily abandon an unsuccessful experiment.

The Autumn term had hardly started when I fell ill with paratyphoid fever. Infectious illnesses, especially in children, were common at this time and often caused permanent disablement. Measles could cause deafness. Whooping cough or bronchitis could keep a child away from school for a whole term. Diphtheria or scarlet fever meant transfer to the 'fever' hospital. Consumption (tuberculosis), although the treatment of it had improved and fewer died of it, was still dreaded.

My mother's half-brother, John, developed it at the age of twenty and died a few years later. In Matfield village the son of a building contractor had it and spent all his days and nights in an open-sided wooden hut in the garden.

In my first term at school, at morning assembly prayers, Miss East asked all the girls to rise in memory of a 17-year-old pupil, Kathleen Chiesman, who had died of pneumonia. I told Nannie about it that night adding: 'Of course she was quite old'. I was surprised when Nannie replied that 17 was 'little more than a child'.

I had never been really ill before and had always been jealous of the attention Anne received when she had her bad colds and coughs. Now with paratyphoid fever I was the centre of attention but felt so bad that I couldn't enjoy it. The fire burned red all day in the little grate in my bedroom and my father would sit by my bed. Sometimes the doctor from Brenchley, who treated us all free because my father was a war hero, would be in the room. Then a nurse arrived, wearing a strange green uniform. She was a London Hospital nurse, where my father had trained. One of his old friends, a consultant at the hospital, was either paying her wages or had arranged for the hospital to do so.

One day I was able to get up and sit in a chair by the fire with a shawl round me. Then, on a bright spring morning, I was wrapped up warmly and taken for a walk by Nurse. To my dismay she appeared in a little green straw bonnet and a long green cloak that reached the ground. This was, of course, the London Hospital uniform, but I found it altogether too conspicuous. She would have liked to walk to the village but I urged her to take me to the lake. This was a short walk by footpath past the oasthouses and through the apple orchards belonging to Mr Punnett. I thought we wouldn't meet anyone, and we didn't.

I was sent to Brighton with Nurse for a week's convalescence. Although it was a relief to be away from anyone who might recognise me, accompanied by a lady dressed like Florence Nightingale, I recollect that I spent most of the week sulking, which was a very poor reward for her kindness.

When I was fit enough to return to school I found an arrangement had been made for me to live at The Homestead with my grandparents from Monday to Friday so that I would be saved the tiring bus journey. The Homestead was ten minutes walk from the school. A girl of my own age lived nearby and called for me every morning. She introduced me to the thrilling adventure of ringing door bells and running away. Thus living in Tunbridge Wells was both exciting and boring. The door bells were exciting; coming home to The Homestead was not. Food was always substantial. Sometimes I found it difficult to eat at all; I still hadn't much appetite and had strong 'fads', as grandmother called them. I didn't like ginger or gooseberries and quite a few other items designated as 'wholesome'.

There was a large oil painting I liked in the dining room. It was called 'Venice' and depicted a number of women with their skirts rolled up standing knee-deep in water with washtubs in their arms. One or two carried babies instead of washtubs. It was an extraordinary picture, the strangest view of Venice, if indeed the artist had ever been to Venice, that I have ever seen. But it was a much pleasanter picture than 'The Death of General Wolfe' on the stairs.

After lunch grandmother would go out, dressed fashionably, often in a fur coat, to play bridge. Grandfather would go into his 'den' and fall asleep in a leather armchair.

Bored, I would sometimes go into the garden and look at the white marble swans on the edge of the pond. I was attracted to an enclave of hurdles at the end of a neat gravel path and very disappointed to find it housed the refuse bins.

Grandfather would wake up at tea time and the maid would serve us tea on a little table in the den. There was a comfortable smell of tobacco and bulb fibre, for he was a pipe-smoker and used to prepare bowls of hyacinths on a bench grandmother had had especially erected.

One day, he noticed I was crying and drew me towards him. 'What's the matter?', he said.

'It's prize-giving at school at the end of the week and all the girls will have white frocks except me.'

'Well,' he said, 'I've a surprise for you. Your mother is calling here tomorrow with your dress.'

I did have a white dress for prize-giving, but I am quite sure it was arranged by grandfather, probably with grandmother's co-operation. My mother would have been very unlikely to have remembered the note about dress which doubtless had been sent by the school to all parents.

17 – HOLIDAYS

'Daughters of gentlemen' – *Formamints* – *superstitions* – *cast-offs from Fortnum & Mason, Harrods* – *tennis parties* – *school clothes* – *tonsils.*

The holidays had just started at the end of my second year at the High School when I was told that I was to go to a new school at the beginning of the autumn term.

Grandmother Willett had become aware that the daughter of a friend's chauffeur went to the High School, the daughter of the chemist in the High Street (which might have been just acceptable), and the daughter of the gentlemans' outfitter patronised by grandfather (which was not).

So it was suggested that, with the promise of a small increase to my father's allowance, I should be sent to St Clair, on Frant Road, Tunbridge Wells, a private school advertised 'for daughters of gentlemen'. This must have been particularly appropriate, since the occupation of 'father' on my birth certificate is given as 'gentleman'.

I cannot remember that I made a fuss about leaving the High School and my friends, probably because I was told at the beginning of the Summer holidays; the autumn term seemed a long way ahead and, meanwhile, it was summer. The mist in the early morning, the scent of the roses, the colours in my father's herbacious border, the strawberries ripening under the nets in the vegetable garden – all this and much more filled me with joyful expectancy peculiar to childhood. Moreover, I had my first bicycle, too big and second-hand, but I was allowed to ride to the village shops on it.

Some of the village people smiled and waved at me as I passed them on the road, though others were aloof. The district nurse, for example, granite-faced, in a dark blue coat and close-fitting cap used to ride past without looking at me. Nannie told me that she was offended because my mother had had a living-in nurse for Anne's birth and she would have liked to have been asked to attend.

Miss Selina Storr always smiled brightly and was very kind, as I found out: I had been given an errand to the village by my mother which required a visit to the Post Office, now moved from its solitary magnificence in the front room of the little cottage next door to Miss Reeves to Newbolds, one of the three village grocers. The path sloped down to the door of Newbolds from the road. Instead of getting off my bicycle and walking down the path, I attempted to ride. There was a terrific crash as I hit the door, which flew open. The bike came to rest on the floor of the shop with me on top of it. I was both frightened and hurt, although I don't remember crying. I was picked up by Miss Selina Storr with Mrs Newbold tut-tutting behind the counter. 'You must have that nasty cut seen to', she observed, looking at the blood pouring from the leg. So that was how I found myself in the dining room of Matfield Court having my leg bandaged by Miss Selina while Miss Eleanor held a bowl of warm water and a sponge.

New people, the Hubbards, had taken Matfield House. They had three children. At Christmas, Denis and I had been asked to a children's party and were able to inspect, with much wonderment, their magnificent nursery, schoolroom and toys. The summer holidays had just begun when I met the children and their nurse as I was riding past the green. Ever anxious to make friends I got off my bicycle and spoke to them. They didn't seem very responsive, and, disappointed, I rode on. Later on, Mrs Hubbard telephoned to say they were in quarantine for mumps, so I was roundly scolded by my mother who always had a unreasoning fear of 'infection', which might be passed on to my father. For this reason, she usually had a bottle of lozenges, called Formamints, in her bag which we were always given to suck if, for example, we were about to travel by bus or train.

She was very superstitious. In her nature realism and fatalism were often struggling for supremacy. If she defied fate by walking under a ladder, sitting 13 at a table, turning a mattress on Friday, then some dreaded event would come to pass. The conclusive endorsement of her irrationality was that my father had been wounded on 13 December. Now no event could take place on the 13th of the month. My father was unusually patient with her and once agreed that a bookcase he wanted, which arrived on the 13th, should be put in the coalhouse overnight. She had wondered whether this would be enough to ward off bad luck, but to leave it under the old pear tree, where it would get wet if it rained, seemed not a sensible alternative.

Mrs Cheeseman, the daily help, ordered not to turn the mattresses on Friday, soon saved herself trouble by never turning them at all. My hair mattress gradually shaped itself into a hollow. I grew so used to it that I was uncomfortable if I slept on a flat mattress.

Denis had brought a canoe home from school. He had made the frame with the help of the carpentry master, and the village carpenter had stretched canvas over it.

One morning, he woke me up at six o'clock. We crept downstairs and tied the canoe on top of the wheelbarrow. Denis promised that I should have the first turn in it. We set out for the village pond in the misty early morning. The flimsy craft rocked violently as he pushed it out from the bank, and there was a big splash as it turned over and I stood in water up to my waist. But Denis' concern was for the canoe. We hauled it out between us and put it on the wheelbarrow. Some of the canvas flapped loose and Denis said it would have to be mended before it went in the water again. My dripping wet clothes and shoes that squelched at every step made the return journey uncomfortable but we met only Johnson, the postman, who gave us a cheery wave as he rode past with his brown canvas mail bag over his shoulder.

Shortly after the canoe disaster came the annual visit from Auntie Vi and Uncle Leslie Finnis and their two daughters, Daphne and Rosemary. They always arrived in a chauffeur-driven car before lunch, played tennis in the afternoon, and left after tea. The Finnis girls were two or three years older than I was and always wore beautiful clothes.

The boxes of cast-off clothes which arrived twice a year from 19 Brechin Place, Kensington, the Finnis' home, were the most substantial help my aunt ever gave her sister. At birthdays and Christmas my mother received six pairs of silk stockings. But the clothes from Fortnum & Masons and Harrods enabled my sister and me to be far better dressed than we would otherwise have been. Grandmother Willett only once bought me a dress when I stayed for a few days at the Leas Hotel, Folkestone, with her and grandfather. I liked it, but out of loyalty preferred to wear the smocked dress which Nannie had made for me.

That summer (1927) I wore to church a pale blue organdie dress with sprigs of forget-me-nots embroidered on it. The sash was blue, pink and white satin ribbons. The expensive hat I wore was cream straw, lined under the brim with ruched pink silk. The crown was encircled with a garland of artificial flowers, rosebuds, forget-me-nots and daisies. My feelings about this hat were totally out of proportion. Quite simply, I adored it. It could not have suited Rosemary, for it seemed to be unworn.

The preparations for the Finnis visit always commenced the evening before, with my mother dusting and polishing in the drawing room. I liked to help by polishing the gate-leg table in the dining room and cleaning the brass taps in the bathroom with Brasso. On the morning of the visit, Mrs Cheeseman's heavy tread could be heard in the kitchen, and the clanking as she pulled out the oven damper and stoked up the fire in the kitchen range. Meanwhile I was in the garden picking sweet peas and raspberries. The sweet peas were not picked for a week beforehand, so I was always able to pick a huge bunch, grading the colours carefully, palest mauve to deep purple, deep red to palest pink.

The menu for lunch was always the same: roast leg of lamb, peas from the garden and new potatoes, followed by raspberries and cream. Water was the only drink.

A row of deck chairs were set out beside the tennis court, newly mown and marked out. About half past two other guests, local friends, arrived for tennis and tea. Children were never allowed on the court, except when the guests were having tea. Then we rushed on the court with old balls and the misshapen racquets my father had used at Cambridge. The Finnis girls had new 'junior' racquets.

During August, my mother took me to Miss Childs to be measured for my new school dresses. The dresses would have to be ready on our return from the family holiday in September. The High School uniform was a gym tunic with a white blouse, viyella in winter, cotton in summer. Black shoes and stockings, wool in winter, lisle in summer, and a school tie completed the daily uniform. For outdoors, a navy blue reefer coat and black velour hat in winter and a panama hat and blazer in summer were both practical and relatively inexpensive. Navy blue knickers with a pocket for a handkerchief and white inner cotton linings were worn by all pupils in both the junior and upper schools.

St Clair, my new school, had a much longer clothing list, over which my mother pored anxiously, no doubt wondering how to devise the least expensive way of meeting the requirements. My navy blue school tunic with braid girdle would do until it was outgrown, and the viyella blouses and black velour hat. St Clair pupils wore black ties and no hatband. At lunchtime (my mother read), after games, all girls had to change into blue serge dresses, in winter with white collars. In summer, they had to change into blue alpaca dresses with white collars until half-term, when blue cotton dresses, the material purchased at Weekes Department Store in Tunbridge Wells, could be worn, made in any plain pattern with white collars. Outdoor walking shoes must always be changed for indoor shoes with a strap. The High School panama hat would have to be discarded in favour of navy blue straw hats. And a summer navy serge coat was compulsory.

I was to have new winter coat; the hated cut-down one had been outgrown at last. Although it was tedious to stand still while Miss Childs swooped around me with her mouth full of pins, I enjoyed the visits. Her tiny work-room, which was also the sitting room, was dominated by a huge painting on one wall of a horse being shoed at the village forge with a little girl in a bonnet standing by. I was intensely fond of this romantic picture, probably a copy of a famous painting.

Sadly, Miss Childs didn't own her cottage. It belonged to the Storrs. When her old father died in the 1930's she was given notice as the Storrs had built a new house next door and wanted the cottage for a retainer. Miss Childs moved into a council house in the village and the picture went with her, looking as incongruous as its owner in the ugly dwellings which the council inflicted on the village. She lived to 90.

In the later part of August, 1927, Denis and I were taken to the Eye and Ear Hospital on Mount Sion, Tunbridge Wells to have our adenoids and tonsils removed. This was a horrible experience. The fright and shock of seeing the operating theatre with its grisly tray of instruments and white-coated, masked figures was bad enough. Worse was to have a mask pressed over my face and to sense the sweet smell of chloroform. I had a moment of terror before I lost consciousness. Would they use the knife while I was still awake? I tried to shout for them not to do it, but, as I opened my eyes, I was back in the hospital ward with a painful sore throat. And instead of a pillow there was a sticky mackintosh sheet.

The only pleasant experience in hospital was that I tasted ice cream for the first time.

I suppose we were in hospital for only a few days, but the day before we went out grandmother arrived in the ward with matron, graciously smiling. She had come to take us for a drive in Ashdown Forest. Never did we enjoy a drive in grandmother's Rover so much.

18 — THE BROADS

Competition between buses — our first car — loan of holiday home — early motoring — Jack is lost, and found — life on the Broads — the bittern boom — Roland Green.

In 1928 two bus companies operated in Matfield: the Redcar and the Autocar. They plied between Cranbrook, an old Kentish wool town, and Tunbridge Wells, passing through Goudhurst, dominated by its beautiful old church in the middle of the village, Horsmonden, Brenchley (another wool town), Matfield, Pembury and Tunbridge Wells.

Nannie was staunch supporter of Redcar and would never travel in anything else. Redcars were supposed to be the more refined type of bus, their colour a discreet maroon. Autocars were thought to be 'common'. They were bright green. Competition between the two companies was brisk. They both had regular supporters, like Nannie, who would prefer to wait at the bus stop rather than enter an Autocar. The Redcar and Autocar rivalry benefited all villagers who were not deeply committed to either bus, for fares fell very low as each strove for passengers. There was always an attempt to pirate each other's timetables by running a bus a few minutes before the rival company. The drivers of the buses were not averse to trying to pass each other to reach the next picking-up point first. On one occasion an Autocar forced a Redcar into a ditch. This incident caused something of a local scandal. So the rivalry moderated to safer practices, like cheaper return fares.

When I first went to the High School competition between the buses was very intense. Sometimes I could get to Monson Road, Tunbridge Wells, to catch the Redcar to Matfield, but when I missed it I was in a dilemma, for the Autocar ran four minutes later. I endured surprised stares of Matfield inhabitants as I remained at the bus stop when everyone else had got on. The next Redcar was forty minutes later. This was the last time I

100

waited for the Redcar. Nannies's feelings couldn't be hurt, I thought, if she didn't see me getting off an Autocar; the official bus stop was Matfield Grove, fifty yards beyond The Rosery.

Although the coming of the buses meant that my father was not confined to the village for his bird-watching and natural history, as he had been since Tommy's departure three years earlier, cars were now on the road in increasing numbers.

After some optimistic calculations on running costs (petrol was 11 pence a gallon) my father purchased an old Armstrong Siddeley tourer for £15, and my mother learned to drive. It had a canvas folding roof and side screens made of celluloid. When they cracked, as they often did, they had to be mended with glue and transparent paper.

1928 was the first summer we had a car and we were going to Norfolk in it for the first fortnight in September. Nannie was to stay at home, for the kind of holiday we were to have would not have suited her. Nor would it have suited my father to have her. She liked a settled routine and did not spare her grumbles if it was broken into.

A Cambridge friend of my father, Reginald Winder, had purchased, or leased, an acre of land on Hickling Broad, Norfolk, including water frontage. On this he moored a large houseboat and nearby erected a wooden hut about 15 feet square. This holiday home was called The Camp and was approached by a long footpath, winding between swampy ground, from the Pleasure Boat Inn at the village end of the wide stretch of water. The Winder family usually spent August on Hickling, but for several years they offered it to my father for a family holiday in September.

At the beginning of September we set off from The Rosery early in the morning, three children in the back, two pekinese dogs, our heads almost hitting the car roof because we had to sit on sheets, towels, coats spread along the back seat. One big trunk, filled to bursting point with clothes, was tied on the luggage rack at the back, with two dog baskets on top. As the day was fine it was decided to lower the hood, which certainly made it more comfortable for the passengers.

I suppose we must have travelled at twenty-five to thirty miles an hour. Even so, it seemed a long time before we reached Gravesend and my mother drove the car slowly onto the big ferry boat. The holiday seemed already to have begun as we stood at the rail, watching the boats chugging along this wide stretch of the Thames. When the ferry reached Tilbury we were off again for Ipswich. Although there were not many cars on the narrow roads we had a makeshift flag, a scarf on the end of a walking stick which we hoisted when we headed a queue of perhaps three or four. Inmates of cars that passed us smiled and waved as we lowered the flag.

When it was time for lunch my mother drew into the verge beside a field and we all retreated modestly behind trees. Then I noticed that the black pekinese, Jack, was missing. Frenzied search of the car, underneath the clothes, underneath the seats, failed to reveal him. It became clear that he had jumped or fallen out of the car, probably during one of the flag-raising ceremonies, when he would have been unobserved.

We all feared that Jack had gone for ever, but my mother turned the car and drove slowly back along the road. To everyone's joy we saw a farm labourer walking along the road carrying him. He had picked Jack up from the ditch, he said, and had been bitten for his pains. He intended to take Jack to the police station in the next village thinking that surely someone would miss such a pretty little dog.

In the late afternoon we arrived at Stalham, the nearest small town to Hickling Broad, and bought the provisions to last the next few days. There was no refrigerator in The Camp (nor, of course, at The Rosery); so more tins than perishable foods were required.

Milk was available at the Pleasure Boat Inn, jugs filled, as at home, from a big churn with the pewter measures hung on the side. Every morning my brother or I punted the boat round from The Camp to collect the milk.

Once in The Camp, which necessitated several journeys carrying belongings from the car, drinking water had to be fetched. The Camp had two boats, a punt and a rowing boat. My father could manage only one oar but punted skilfully with one hand. He punted the boat through the dyke, an avenue some ten feet wide cut between the reeds, which, even then, encroached some fifty feet into Hickling Broad. After some distance to clear water we lowered a bucket and drew it up, full. This task took place every day, for the water had to be boiled and then, the odd brackish taste concealed with lime juice, it was ready for drinking.

The Broad was too deep in the centre (the channel marked with posts) for the punt, so the rowing boat was used for expeditions across the water, either Denis or I pulling the oars with my father. For £1 a week we hired an old boat with a sail, which would have been more fun if the winds had been brisker and the boat not so heavy. Often we moved at a snail's pace while newer, lighter boats with two sails whisked past us. One of these contained a family known to my parents from pre-War days. Mrs Wimble, dressed in white with a fashionable hat, reclining on cushions as her husband and two young sons managed the boat, would lean over and call to us, always the same words, 'Lovely, isn't it?' We named her 'Lovely'. As my father struggled to catch the wind in our flapping sail, my mother would say, 'Lovely's coming up the channel'. Motor boats and outboard engines were much disliked by my father, both for the noise which would frighten the birds and the oil might clog their wings. His binoculars were always slung round his neck and sometimes he would moor the boat for an hour or two, waiting for a rare bird to fly from the reeds.

One morning we all were out of bed at dawn. My father wanted us to hear the bittern booming. It was a clear morning, the air still and rather cold. This, or a calm evening at sunset, he said was the most likely time to hear the astonishing call of this heron-like bird. As we listened, he spoke to us quietly about the writings of Sir Thomas Browne, 1605-1682, doctor, writer, naturalist, author of *A Doctor's Religion*. Then, amidst the calls of other water birds, we heard the distinctive boom. It was a most thrilling moment.

'It's wonderful to imagine that we are hearing the same sound as Sir Thomas Browne,' said my father. 'In his time this part of England and many others would have been a vast swamp. The population was such smaller. There were many bitterns, a bird which in the last hundred years nearly became extinct.'

Some days, when we were sailing slowly along the network of waterways radiating on Hickling, we would see one of the most beautiful sights we had ever seen, a large Norfolk wherry with full sail making its majestic way between the banks of reeds.

My father had spent several boyhood holidays on the Norfolk Broads, sent to a rectory by his parents so that he could enjoy his favourite pastimes: filling up notebooks with his observations about birds and plant life, fishing and shooting. The Rector had a fine knowledge of birds, derived from a lifetime's hobby. He was a sportman and a man who revelled in wild weather and wild places. Observations of birds, flowers, weather and country doings and sayings he wrote down for over forty years. Natural history journals published some of his papers.

My father admired him immensely and learned much from him. Years after his death he talked about the rector with an old eel-catcher, in his hut on the river bank while his nets were down:

'He was the best man that ever lived round here', said the seventy-year-old fisherman, 'and a good sportsman too. I remember many years ago, I'd shot a black-winged tern which I knew was about on the Broad, for I wanted the money that winter; work was short, and I'd been promised a pound by a gentleman if I could being him a 'black wing'. I picked it up; it was a beautiful thing, and I thought I could be away with it before the keeper came; and then I saw the Rector in his punt in the reeds. He'd been watching a nest. 'Oh, mister,' I said, 'I hope you don't tell on me', for I knew he was a friend of the owner, and moreover black-winged terns were on the protected list all the year round. But he says, shaking his head at me, 'Bob, I've done too many things I'm ashamed of, that were never found out, to tell on you even if I thought I could withstand your temptation'. You see, he knew how poor we were that winter.'

On one of his first visits to the Broads, after the War, my father visited the Rectory, only to find that the house had been burned down, the old rector and his wife were dead, their two sons killed in the war and their daughter, Kate, whom my father had loved passionately when they were both eighteen, had been married and died in child-birth during the War. Sadly, my father sought their graves in the little churchyard. He stood by Kate's grave and wondered again why so many friends of his youth and boyhood had been taken from the world in their springtime. How fortunate he had been that, loving Kate so much in his early youth, he had found a dearer love and married her.

My father had an old friend, Roland Green, a bird artist of growing reputation, who lived in an old houseboat on a stretch of the river, flowing from Hickling Broad. His father had been a bricklayer and he had had only elementary education. He taught himself to draw and watch birds in flight. Soon his skill in portraying rocketing pheasants and grouse, ducks and geese in flight, lapwings and other birds with their young, earned him a wealthy clientele. He could have afforded to live in a more comfortable way, but he, a bachelor, preferred his lonely life by the waterside, absorbed in his drawing and his bird-watching.

My father had long talks with him, not only about birds but also about social conditions which interested them both. Roland Green thought that education was without justice for the poor and without wisdom for the rich, that it left artistic talent unfostered in children of all classes. On this particular occasion they talked together until it grew dark. The moon rose and I was half asleep in the boat moored to his little jetty, waiting to row with my father back to The Camp.

Roland had been asking my father about his writing. My father told him he was writing a novel about the War.

'Why don't you write about birds? You know a tremendous lot about them. Why not have a go?'

'Everybody writes about birds, nowadays,' answered my father despondently.

'Nonsense, most of them are just cribbed. You could do something worth while.'

As we rowed across the water to The Camp together, my father was in a cheerful mood. The ripples on the water were moon-splashed and he recited Keats' 'Ode to Autumn' as I struggled to keep my rowing in time with his.

As we entered the dyke I saw my mother standing on the

landing stage, her hands clasped before her in an attitude of anxiety. Her fears for his safety always roused my father's irritation. The fears were justified enough. He could not have survived an overturned boat. Yet he did not want to be reminded that he was no longer the strong young man who had once swam and rowed on Hickling Broad.

Perhaps because the Norfolk scene reminded him so strongly of his youthful self when his right arm and leg responded to the messages from his brain, when his athletic body met every strain he put on it, he decided to see if he could still swim. He thought he could manage a sideways crawl.

The water surrounding the houseboat was deep. It was clear, and among the reeds were pike — a fish so still that they seemed sinister, especially because they looked like small shark. My father was courageous but not foolhardy. The attempt at swimming would be made in a cove on the Broad where the bottom was stony and hard, the water shallow. Thither we rowed, my father wearing shorts, my mother trying to hide her apprehension. We anchored the boat and he climbed over the side. Using his left arm vigorously, he propelled himself several yards. It was a triumph, but he lay in the bottom of the boat exhausted when he finally gave up and allowed us to pull him over the side.

Bittern and Young

106

19 — NANNIE

The family grows up — Nannie leaves — her new job — Home Notes — Nannie's new home — she returns to Anne — a tribute.

When we got home from Norfolk there were only a few days before Denis would return to the Grange and the Christmas term at St Clair would begin. Nannie was busy in the day nursery sewing name tapes on my new clothes, her stitches so fine they could not be seen. I liked her big sewing basket, so neatly arranged with coloured cottons and silks. I was quite unprepared when she bent her head toward the basket, fumbled in it in an unaccustomed manner, and a tear trickled down her cheek. She took out her handkerchief and stifled a sob.

I had seen my mother cry on one or two occasions and had always been distressed, but never Nannie! Nannie was at this time my anchor post in life. She was always there, sometimes grumpy but dearly beloved. She saw me off to school in the morning, neatly dressed, no holes in stockings, no buttons missing. She served my lunch when I got back from school and then cleared the nursery table for my homework. She was there at night, sleeping in the bed next to mine, getting dressed under her voluminous flannel nightgown in the morning.

She had never been demonstrative to her charges, but the knowledge of her love was there. Now, I put my hand on her shoulder:

'Nannie! Nannie! Why are you crying?'

'I'm leaving. Yes, when you get home from school tomorrow I shan't be here!'

There was a funny sensation in the pit of my stomach.

'Nannie,' I gasped 'I'm going to be sick'.

Always resourceful in emergency, Nannie picked up the baby's pot and held my head while I was sick. Then she helped me onto my bed where I lay looking up into her dear face while the tears streamed from my eyes.

107

'Why are you leaving us?' I asked.

'Denis and you are at school and Baby is starting at Miss Birch's kindergarten in Brenchley. So I'm not needed.'

'But I need you!' I answered, choking with sobs.

I was inconsolable that day. My mother and father looked at me anxiously at teatime but said nothing. They had, as I later saw, made the only decision possible to cut household costs. Nannie was not very willing to help Mrs Cheeseman, and she would be needed less and less for Anne, who was now five. Furthermore, my Grandmother Munt had written that the daughter of a friend wanted a Nannie for her new baby. It would be a good opportunity for Nannie to start again with a young family.

My new clothes for school lay on a chair at the foot of my bed, but all my thoughts that night were desolate. I often used to creep out of bed and take Nannie's weekly magazine, *Home Notes*, out of her top drawer and read the children's page, hurriedly replacing it if I heard footsteps in the corridor. Now the sight of the chest of drawers produced a fresh wave of misery. Everything would be changed.

During the Christmas holidays, when the first edge of grief had worn off, Anne and I were taken to visit Nannie at Battersea, where her new employers had a flat. We went for a walk in Battersea Gardens, Nannie trundling the big marmet pram with the small red-haired baby girl in it. When we returned to the flat, Anne and I sat at the nursery table while Nannie heated milk on the spirit lamp and gave the baby a bottle. Even to my childish perception, it was obvious that Nannie was loving the care of a young baby.

She stayed with this family for nearly twenty years looking after four children. Finally she returned to The Rosery at the end of the Second World War for a visit and remained, permanently, to make my father's tea every afternoon while my mother played bridge. When they died, my sister took her home and she stayed with her, well looked after until the end of her life. So her dedication to other people's children was rewarded by a comfortable old age.

She live to be 90. Although bedridden for the last few years, she was always ready to recite nursery rhymes to Anne's children and mine. Nannie's heaven, and I trust she has found it, would be a cosy nursery with a fire burning in the grate, a fireguard with a brass rail, several little children, and a gramophone playing 'Polly, Put the Kettle on'.

Nannie was pre-eminently a Kensington Garden kind of nannie. She was very royalist, and when Princess Elizabeth was born in 1926 she had acute pleasure in following the progress of the royal baby. If we had lived in London, she would have enjoyed gossiping with other nannies in the royal parks, with the likely chance of meeting the two royal nannies, the royal 'marmet' pram and the royal baby along the then uncrowded walks of Kensington Gardens.

Duck

20 – ST CLAIR

Miss Vickery: owner/headmistress – 'Harold' – from day-girl to boarder – reduced fees – no fees for Jewish refugees – The Sleeping Beauty – As You Like It – table rules – consideration for residents.

St Clair was a small school, with forty day-girls and twenty boarders. A big red-brick Victorian mansion, half way up Frant Road, Tunbridge Wells, was the school-house.

The school was owned by a lady, then in her sixties, called Miss Caroline Esmé Deprez Vickery. She was the headmistress, but ran the school with a lady of strong personality, Miss Violet Hamnet. Vick and Ham, as they were known by everyone, shared their domestic life.

The front door of the school-house opened into a spacious hall with the drawing room, study and a large dining room, off it. This area was out of bounds to girls, except by special invitation. Behind the green baize door was the school room, used for prayers, but with sliding wooden doors to convert it into two classrooms. The front stairs were not used by the pupils. The back stairs led to the classrooms. There were four classrooms and the science room on the first floor, and Miss Vickery's bedroom. No pupil had ever seen inside this room. A bathroom and Matron's 'den' were also on this floor. A short flight of stairs, on one side of the house, led to the maids' attic bedrooms; and on the other side of the house a similar flight of stairs led to three bedrooms and a bathroom for the junior boarders.

The school-house had a side door leading out of the day girls' cloakroom to a flight of stone steps connecting the school-house with the senior boarding house. Twelve girls and Miss Hamnet and Matron slept in this house, and the sick room adjoined Matron's bedroom. The house was very cold; the only heating was a boiler for the water. In winter, the mistress on duty would sit in the boiler room huddled in a coat.

110

The third big house owned by the school was next to the boarders' house. The two rooms on the ground floor were used as a kindergarten and art room. The four living-in teachers, or 'mistresses' as we called them, occupied the rest of the house.

The three gardens of the houses were not separated and gravel paths ran round them. The boarding house had a tennis court which became a netball pitch in winter. There was no playground and in break girls strolled round the paths in twos and threes. Arm-in-arm walking was not permitted, nor was running. The wooden seats encircling the big trees might be used in summer but not in winter.

I started my first school term in the third form. The classroom was upstairs, in the front of the house. There were eight girls in the form. A girl with long pigtails, tied with navy ribbon, who said her name was 'Meg', asked me to sit next to her and helped me collect one of the eight piles of exercise books and text books laid out on the teacher's table. Meg lived near the school. (Fifteen years later, her brother, Lionel Queripel, won the Victoria Cross at Arnhem.) My desk was older, more scratched and much bigger than the one I had used at the High School.

No sooner had I sat down than there was a tremendous noise of a gong banging in the corridor. I followed Meg downstairs for prayers. It was the task of the last girl leaving the room to raise the sash window, thus allowing blasts of cold air to cool the room.

Prayers at St Clair were less formal than I had been used to at the High School. Miss Vickery sat at the teacher's table with the Bible open in front of her. She read for ten minutes, usually from the New Testament. Then we all joined in the recitation of the Lord's Prayer. I had known the words before I first read them at the age of six, when I found that God was not, as I had supposed, called 'Harold'. Many children down the years must have misheard 'Hallow'd be thy name.' After prayers, Miss Vickery announced the names of the new Head Girl and Prefects. Some big girls got up and took their privileged seats in a row of chairs facing the assembly.

Our form-mistress taught geography and went to all the other classrooms to teach her subjects. For science, we went to the

111

science room. Here we had fun with bunsen burners, but the subject was not taught very seriously, and was finally abandoned in the run-up to the school certificate examination.

Miss Vickery taught scripture and grammar. Scripture was interesting because she told us about the early history of the Jewish people and their life under Roman rule. She made the New Testament stories much clearer by showing us pictures of Bethlehem, the Dead Sea, the Mount of Olives and other sacred places. I looked forward to her lessons. But grammar was not my favourite subject. We had parsing books; Miss Vickery wrote a sentence on the blackboard and we had to dissect it into adverbs, nouns, verbs and adjectives. Clauses I couldn't understand at all. We had copy books, with lines of Miss Vickery's beautiful pointed copper plate writing. At the High School I had been taught to write in round script, and although I tried to adapt it to Miss Vickery's writing the results were a failure.

I was still very unhappy about Nannie's departure but at school there was no time to think about it. The banging of the gong at forty-minute intervals, the chatter and friendliness of the other girls, the different methods of teaching from those of the High School, endlessly changing shoes — outdoor to indoor, indoor to games, games to indoor, the encouraging discovery that I was good at netball, lunch in the brown dining room (the green dining room was for the senior school), lessons again at 2.15 to 4.o'clock; there was certainly no time to brood at school. But in the bus on the way home my spirits fell. By the time I got home, I was again miserable.

I now had my own bedroom, on the corner of the house, one window facing toward the road and the other looking across the field to The Pines where my Godmother, Miss Stagg, lived. My bedroom gave me great pleasure. Treasures: my tortoiseshell brush, my box made of shells, the framed picture of a little girl kneeling by a bed which Nannie had given me — I placed them all on my chest of drawers. My father had promised to make me a bookcase for my small collection of books. One of the small window panes had a name and date scratched on it 'Nellie Argent, 1867'. I often wondered what she was like: Nellie, the girl who had slept in my bedroom sixty years before.

112

I should have been happy. My mother and father were giving me a lot of attention and I was becoming more conscious of my love for them. Yet at night I developed a curious fantasy that if I fell asleep I would never wake up again. I did sleep, but the strain of trying to keep awake made me feel tired in the morning. There were other incidents. Anne now slept alone in the night nursery, and twice I woke to find I was lying on the floor near her bed, having no recollection of leaving my own bed.

I didn't tell my parents about my strange fancies and sleep-walking but that I was moping must have been obvious. They were worried. They found the solution: I was told that after the half-term holiday I was to become a boarder at St Clair.

More new clothes and more visits to Miss Childs, this time to make a red velvet frock to be changed into after school tea and blue cotton overalls which had to be worn over afternoon dresses by all junior boarders.

I found I was to share a bedroom with two girls, Bobbie Leslie Melville who was in my form, and Nancy Leir who was in Form IV. I was very excited. Now nine years old, I had started to read school stories and felt I was moving into the world of Angela Brazil and Elinor Brent-Dwyer, writers of popular stories for girls in the early decades of this century. I had just finished a story in which the heroine had bravely climbed up a fifty-foot pole to fix the school flag which had been struck by lightning on the eve of Sports Day. She fixed the flag, lost her hold and was falling – no, she was not falling, she was jumping! Outflung arms caught her and a rousing cheer went up from the assembled girls. This ridiculous story so impressed me that I longed for a similar incident which would show my heroism. However, not only had St Clair no flagpole; I also didn't like heights and had difficulty in overcoming my fear at fire practice when a descent down a rope ladder had to be made three flights up from a small iron platform.

One of the few things I disliked about school was the obligatory sewing sessions. The school had a charity bazaar every December in nearby King Charles the Martyr Church Hall, when the work of the sewing classes were sold together with other handwork donated by the girls and their parents.

113

I was so bad at needlework that I was never given anything interesting to do. Hemstitching towels was considered easy and over this I laboured daily, a martyr certainly to Dr Barnardo's and the British and Foreign Bible Society which shared the proceeds of the bazaar. Miss Vickery used to tell us that any girl from St Clair who ventured into the H.Q. of the British and Foreign Bible Society in London would be welcomed with open arms.

Sometimes the sewing sessions were enlivened by an invitation to a class to Miss Vickery's drawing room. She would read aloud to us. I remember shedding so many tears over Uncle Tom's Cabin that I could no longer see the towel I was stitching. It must have been one such afternoon that I, who as a child suffered from embarrassingly unpredictable and all too frequent attacks of cystitis, had an accident while sitting in one of Miss Vickery's armchairs. Nobody noticed the damp patch on the chair as the class was dismissed, but I spent a restless night fearing that I would be expelled.

All day I waited for a summons which never came. Nothing was ever said, and I presume this to have been one of Miss Vickery's characteristic acts of charity. She was a true Christian. I know she took a number of girls, including me, at very much reduced fees. I have wondered since what she must have thought of my grandmother driving round Tunbridge Wells in her chauffeur-driven car while she was giving charity to her granddaughter!

Miss Vickery, later in my schooldays, in about 1933 or 1934, took two Jewish girls whose parents had got them out of Germany before themselves committing suicide. She can have received no payment for these girls, who were brilliant gymnasts and talented dancers. The older sister had blonde hair and blue eyes, the younger was dark and handsome. As was to be expected, their physical abilities were much admired and they became two of the most popular girls in the school.

The maths teacher, Miss Dudeney, sowed seeds of numeracy to flourish in the most unfertile ground. Miss Dudeney lived in Southborough near Tunbridge Wells with her old mother. She arrived by bus every day at 8.45 and caught the 4.o'clock bus

114

home. Her life must have been one of unrelieved dullness. Either she never had a new coat, hat or dress, or the new ones were exact replicas of the old. Her kindness and patience were beyond all praise. When occasionally she found pupils who really liked maths, as I did, she was as pleased if she had received a priceless gift.

She also taught Latin. But here, later in my schooldays, I was not one of her best pupils. My good memory of the translations of Virgil and Caesar she gave us was sufficient to give me a medium placing in class but I knew she was disappointed in me. I can still translate such well-known tags as 'Omnia Gallia in tres partes divisa est', but I never acquired a grasp of the language.

Miss Hamnet was a gifted teacher of English and History. She was not a university graduate but a Shakespeare scholar nonetheless. Twice a year she produced plays. Once she had chosen her cast, everyone had to be word perfect by the first rehearsal. She would bully and push the girls around, shout at them, even shake them, until a true portrayal of the part, as she saw it, was achieved.

In my first summer term, Miss Hamnet produced *The Sleeping Beauty* for the junior school, using the garden as an auditorium. I was given a small part, the Prince. The school dressmaker, who bore a chance resemblance to Miss Childs, made the costumes. I had a black sateen tunic with high collar. One of the older girls made my crown of cardboard, covered in gold paper and with gelatine sweets ('jewels') stuck all round it. I had never acted before. Although I was word-perfect with my lines I felt nervous as I waited in the vegetable garden for my entrance on stage through the opening of the tall box hedge, the 'thicket', to greet the Princess, asleep on a draped camp bed under the oak tree.

In the following year Miss Hamnet produced *As You Like It*. This time I was a forester with nothing to do except wave my bow and arrow and join in the singing. Miss Hamnet had taken the hint about my talent as an actress.

My first winter at school was very cold. In the morning the ewers of water in our bedroom were frozen over. A maid brought up a jug of hot water and dumped it inside the door. We would bound out of bed, shivering in the cold air — the windows, of course, were open at night — and share the hot water between three of us.

Breakfast was substantial enough to warm us up, although the dining room was cold; one small coal fire barely heated the big room. Porridge was followed by an egg or sausage. Then doorstep slices of white bread spread with marmalade were passed round. The rule was to scrape off the marmalade and use it for the slices of bread and butter on plates down the centre of the long table. I think this odd custom must have been a relic from Miss Vickery's own Victorian schooldays.

There was a coal fire in every classroom but its chief beneficiary was the mistress who sat at the table with her back to it. The heat hardly penetrated to the row of desks, and my fingers were often white and numb with cold. Yet this discomfort was nothing compared to the misery of girls with chilblains.

Two meal-time rules were strictly enforced. French had to be spoken at lunch, and no-one must ask for food to be passed to her. The language rule did not have a marked effect on my fluency in French conversation; but the politeness rule, which obliged every girl to look after her neighbours, was one of those lessons that are remembered always.

I felt sorry for day-girls who went home at four o'clock, missing the jolly and noisy tea — where in addition to the bread and jam provided by the school, there might be a cake provided by Adelaide, a fat but pretty girl, a year younger than I. She was so homesick that she was always in tears, and to console her, every week her mother sent a large cake which she shared out at teatime. This generosity should have made her popular, but did not. She was slow to laugh and was not good at games; sympathy for her tears rapidly dwindled. Poor Adelaide was always left till last when sides were picked for games, a humiliating position which I always dreaded would fall to me for I was not a fast runner nor a good athlete.

When it was too wet for games, walks were compulsory. Crocodiles of girls dressed in gumboots and mackintoshes and carrying umbrellas were regularly sighted by local residents. Everyone at St Clair knew the way to Eridge, to Southborough, to Frant and to Hawkenbury, all about three miles away. I don't

116

think anyone enjoyed the walks, least of all the mistress trailing behind with two of the dullest girls — the ones who had not found other partners. If there was a deluge, walks would be off and games organised in the schoolroom. This was the outcome profoundly hoped for by us all — a cloudburst before we'd got our gumboots on. On fine days in winter, the school trooped off with hockey sticks to the Kent County Cricket ground. It was a good hockey pitch but the groundsman was apt to forbid play if rain had fallen in the morning to preserve the turf for summer cricket.

On Sundays we would set out for church dressed in white coats and hats. The shortest way to St Marks was along Broadwater Down, and this was the route taken by Miss Vickery and Miss Hamnet. Miss Vickery considered that the quiet Sunday morning walk to church of Tunbridge Wells residents would be disturbed by a crocodile of chattering girls. For this reason we had to walk two miles of a roundabout route and approach St Marks from a quiet lane. Miss Vickery's consideration for older inhabitants of Tunbridge Wells extended to the railway. Girls travelling up to London at the start of school holidays had to leave from Tunbridge Wells West Station to Victoria, which took an hour longer than from the Central Station to Charing Cross. Miss Vickery believed that ladies travelling to London for shopping expeditions would not like girls crowding into their compartments.

To be clever at lessons was not necessarily to be popular. I worked hard, which I took pains to conceal, afraid that I would be labelled a 'swot', but I did like to come first. I was chagrined when in my second year, a new girl, Estelle Pytches, rapidly overtook me in form order and seemed likely to win the form prize which I had hoped for. St Clair was a friendly school, because small, and unkindness was rare. Yet Estelle seemed to invite mockery. She was not pretty and too obviously preferred the approval of the mistresses, which she had, to that of her fellow pupils. She did not join in any mild rule-breaking, kept her desk and pencil box in meticulous order, and always started every lesson with the earnest concentration of an examination candidate. Mild ragging never produced a smile and so became more spiteful. She lived with her grandmother, because her father worked abroad. Her clothes were old-fashioned in pattern although they conformed to the regulation uniform.

I never joined in the teasing, perhaps because I could too readily project myself into the role of victim. But it never occurred to me to object. Her surname inspired the rhymsters: one ditty I remember well was a reference to the knicker legs which frequently drooped below the edge of her gym tunic:

'Estelle Pytches,
Lost her breeches'

was a joke which she would have done better to laugh at, but she pretended not to hear. She was too insensitive, or perhaps too sensitive, for such a clannish school, and when she left after two terms to join her parents in another part of the country no-one was sorry. I now hoped I would win the form prize at the end of the summer term.

Miss Hamnet had a Morris two-seater car with a 'dicky' seat outside at the back. Sometimes she would invite two girls for a drive with her to King Charles Hall, where we had our annual bazaar, or to an event at another school. The car did not exactly flash past the rest of the school walking in crocodile, but it was highly enjoyable at least to bowl past at a sedate speed with our hair streaming out behind us in the wind.

My two years as a boarder were coming to an end. Although Miss Vickery had reduced her fees so drastically that she must have made a financial loss, my parents believed it would be cheaper for me to be a daygirl. Also Anne, now eight years old, was to start at St Clair, although her fees would be higher than at the kindergarten in nearby Brenchley, and she could travel on the bus with me to Tunbridge Wells.

21 – WEDDING AT ST MARGARET'S

*10 bridesmaids – the most beautiful dress – the bride –
a crisis – beef tea and Brand's Essence – water-waving.*

When I was eleven years old, my mother's (step-) sister, Evelyn
Munt, became engaged to a businessman, Denis Clarke. It was
considered to be a good match and a fashionable wedding was
arranged at St Margaret's, Westminster. There were to be ten
bridesmaids, four of them children, my cousin, Rosemary
Finnis, daughter of Auntie Vi, and I were to be among them.

My mother knew that my dress would cost more than she
could afford but it was decided that it would be a gift from Auntie
Vi and Grandmother Willett. It was long, heavy silk crêpe de
chine, cream coloured, with a jacket of the same material in
delphinium blue; blue shoes and a headdress of blue velvet
leaves completed the outfit.

I was taken to London for a fitting of this creation. The smart
salon was very different from Miss Childs' workroom. I had
recently had flu and, as I stood there repeatedly told to keep still,
my head started to swim, the electric light grew fuzzy. The next
scene I remembered was lying on the thick carpet in my
uncompleted finery. Auntie Evelyn, the bride-to-be, was angry
with my mother. She was usually kind, so she was probably
suffering from pre-wedding nerves. She said that a bridesmaid
swooning at the altar was the last thing she wanted. It looked, for
a moment, as though I was not, after all, to wear the most
beautiful dress I had ever had.

But peace was made, my mother promising to 'build me up' –
a favourite phrase – with cups of beef tea and Brand's Essence.

The day before the wedding, my mother, father and I went to
London to stay with Auntie Vi and Uncle Leslie Finnis at 19
Brechin Place, round the corner from Grandmother Munt's old
house at Ashburn Place. Fortunately my father still had a
morning suit given to him by his father when he left Cambridge

119

so that he could pay the conventional morning call on a hostess after a dance or dinner party.

Nannie Finnis (the Nannie in the Finnis household) ruled the nursery, treating Rosemary like a baby, fetching and carrying for her. After lunch she was to take us both to Harrods where an appointment had been made for our hair to be 'water waved'. This method was considered more suitable for children than curling tongs. The hair was shampooed and, while damp, pressed into waves with combs. Rosemary's hair looked pretty with soft waves when the operation was finished, but mine stuck out sideway and wouldn't lie down.

'It's no use,' pronounced the hairdresser, looking sorrowfully at Nannie Finnis. 'We shall have to use the tongs.' So my hair was crimped into corrugated ridges which fortunately had fallen out sufficiently by the morning for my crown of velvet leaves to sit on it comfortably.

After the wedding, which I remember mostly for waiting in the chilly church porch wrapped in one of Rosemary's shawls, my parents and I returned home with the dress in a large cardboard box. I wore it once again at a Christmas party where I was embarrassed to be the only little girl in a long dress, not at all reassured by my mother's view that I looked nicer than anyone.

Family occasions like Evelyn's wedding might have reminded my mother of the contrast between her life and Vi's. Vi's husband, a successful London solicitor, was rich. There was little emotional and no financial conflict in Vi's life. Yet my mother felt no envy. My father filled her life and she was content. She did not look backwards at what might have been if he had not been wounded. Most likely, he would have been on the staff of a London hospital pushing himself to the limit of his resources with a dedication that would have given him little leisure to spend with his family. Yet prosperity would not have altered my mother's happiness in being Wilfred's wife.

22 – GRANDMOTHER MUNT

From wealthy home to aspidistra hotel – horse-race betting –
Auntie Vi's surveillance – Harrogate – her daughters –
ostrich feathers.

My Grandmother Munt was accustomed to visit The Rosery
once a year.

She was now living permanently at the Harrington Hall
Hotel, in Kensington, an aspidistra type of residential home. The
guests were mostly widows or elderly single ladies. On one of
my few visits there it seemed dreary and sad. Grandmother
(born Stenhouse) had come down in the world since her
girlhood. She had been a beautiful girl: her hair was still a rich
reddish brown without a trace of grey. When she died, well over
seventy, she still had no grey hairs. Her sister, Aunt Tottie
(Charlotte), she told me, had been even more beautiful – when
she went to the opera all the ladies and gentlemen raised their
opera glasses to stare at her.

Not only had Grandmother Munt deteriorated in her worldly
circumstances, her income being just enough for the residential
hotel; she had also deteriorated in appearance. Her long hair fell
out of its hairpins, which scattered all over the floor. Her flowing
black skirt was not always spotless, and she made a lot of use of
safety pins. She always carried a capacious bag with tortoiseshell
handles in which she kept, among the general muddle, betting
slips and newspaper cuttings relating to horse races, racing tips,
and the seasonal 'form' of horses.

Betting had been for many years her chief interest in life.
Perhaps this was not surprising, considering her childhood
experience of her father's racing stable. She had – so I heard in
listening to a conversation between my mother and Auntie Vi –
lost thousands of pounds betting while my Grandfather Munt
was alive. Although now severely restricted in income and,
moreover, subjected to surveillance because Auntie Vi lived

near the Harrington Hall Hotel and was able to drop in unannounced and make a clean sweep of all 'horsey' material in Grandmother's bedroom, she obviously still hoped to improve her financial circumstances by a winning bet.

Grandmother had never looked after the six children as they had been tended from birth by nurses and governesses. She herself received devoted care from her own old nurse 'Pepi'. Pepi had waited on her so that she never had to lift a hand to do anything for herself. Her clothes, her hair, domestic worries were all dealt with by Pepi. When she went out visiting or shopping, in her carriage, Pepi was always waiting on her return to help her remove her outdoor clothes and corsets, wrap her in a dressing gown and install her on a sofa in the drawing room.

The great love of her life was her second son, John. When he died of consumption, shortly after the death of Pepi, her world must have fallen apart. Probably it was in the months or years that followed that she distracted herself by betting heavily. Her second husband, dimly remembered by me as kind and patient, no doubt did his best to make her happy by giving her all the money she wanted.

When he died, she was truly alone at last. Auntie Vi was stern with her; her surviving son Raymond lived in the North of England (he played cricket for Yorkshire as an amateur); her other daughters, Vera and Evelyn, she hardly ever saw. She was fond of my mother, who wouldn't leave The Rosery to go to London to visit her; so the annual visit was the only time they saw each other.

Once or twice a year Grandmother went to Harrogate for a treatment to relieve her rheumatism. She often wrote to my mother, the black-edged envelopes in a large distinctive hand, black ink, invariably marked 'URGENT'. The contents were always heavily underlined. I have one of these letters written shortly after arrival in Harrogate marked 'URGENT'. It reads:

Dearest Eileen,

When I arrived at the hotel I found my hatbox was missing. It contained *two* hats, so I have only the *one* I was wearing. I think the porter at St. Pancras must have left it on the platform. I had six boxes and he said *he had put them all in*. But when I got out at Harrogate, the porter could only find *five*. I have spoken to the Station Master, explaining how *upset* I was and he will try and help. Could Wilfred do anything?

Your loving Mother

It must have been very difficult for her to reconcile herself to a lonely life at the Harrington Hall Hotel after years of affluence and comfort, a busy household of six children, an indulgent husband, and many servants. Perhaps my mother would have been more patient with her than was Auntie Vi if she had lived as near for, unlike Vi, she was not irritated by their mother's increasing eccentricity. Vi was ambitious socially. Her daughters were presented at Court: Daphne married the son of the first Baron Hacking, made a peer for his work for the Conservative Party and for tourism; her son married a daughter of Churchill's wartime Chief of Staff, Hastings ('Pug') Ismay. Vi felt the embarrassment of the eccentric old lady. My mother had never been close to Grandmother; although she saw her only rarely, she kept no photograph. Of all her family, except her step-father, whom she had loved, my mother's only fondness was for Vi. She kept a court photograph of Vi with her two daughters, all three wearing ostrich feathers in their hair, in the drawing room. The glass had been cracked when it was knocked over, but my mother still put it out, possibly thinking it would be impressive at bridge parties. My father disliked it, partly because he didn't like bird feathers used as feminine ornaments. But my mother had her own way with pictures in the drawing room, as he did in the study.

23 — 1930

School prizes replaced — books and bookshops — Goulden & Curry — perilous swims — courage and freedom — vegetarianism — animal shoots — edible fungi — war novels unwanted — disillusionment with the church.

During the last two years I had become deeply attached to my father. He took a close interest in all I did at school.

Because St Clair was so small, the competition was not strong and I often won prizes. Usually they were purchased by Miss Vickery from a school books commercial traveller. I was given *British Soldier Heroes*, followed a term later by *British Sailor Heroes* followed by *The Boy's Froissart*, and so on. My father always replaced them with books of his own choosing. I acquired Thomas Hardy's short stories, in this way, W. H. Hudson's *The Purple Land* and others. He always cut out Miss Vickery's prize plate and re-stuck it neatly in the replacement prize.

My father's own books had grown in number since he had come to The Rosery, and now covered two walls of his study from ceiling to floor. He spent many hours in Mr Yeoman's second-hand bookshop in Tunbridge Wells and in another in Chapel Place — where I sometimes used to take a few of my less-prized books on the way to school and sell them for half a crown or five shillings.

His third 'assignation' was with Goulden and Curry, booksellers, in the High Street. Sometimes he bought books but often he came in to discuss a book or writer with Mr Rayward, the manager, and Miss Elizabeth Woodhams, his assistant (who works there to this day). They were never impatient with his lengthy visits. He was one of their best-read customers. Books were their world, and he shared it.

Mr Rayward was tall and wore a patch over one eye. He had a slight stoop that sometimes seemed to make him hover like a large bird over the book-laden table in the centre of the upstairs floor. A newcomer to the shop would immediately be aware of his kindly personality, unfailing courtesy and profound knowledge. For several generations of book-lovers, he *was* Goulden & Curry.

My father usually had a pencilled list of books he currently wanted, and would sometimes give me a copy so I could seek out second-hand bookshops and ask for the books. All one summer I had a list which began with E. M. Forster's *Passage to India*

He was proud of my accomplishment in swimming, for in other respects I was not the athlete he had been. He had taught me to swim in Norfolk. His method of teaching was to tell me to get out of the boat on the waters of Hickling Broad, Norfolk, out of my depth, and then move the boat away with his long punt pole. It was effective, but it scared me. I did become a strong swimmer and, later, when I was ten or eleven, could swim a considerable distance. I enjoyed his pleasure in this achievement. When we went to the sea for the day in the Armstrong Siddeley, usually to a deserted part of the coast, near Dungeness or Folkestone, so that he could observe sea birds, I would swim away from the beach, conscious of his encouragement and the silence of my mother, who no doubt was terrified. I would swim on and on towards the horizon, more and more frightened that I would never get back, hardly daring to look at the blue depths beneath me or, over my shoulder, at the receding beach.

My father's attitude to courage had the advantage that he allowed his children much more freedom than most parents did. We could vanish all day with an improvised fishing rod and sandwiches to the Furnace Pond, a dark and very deep stretch of water near Horsmonden, a few miles away from Matfield, and he would make no effort to forbid the expedition. His philosophy was similar to that of the father in Arthur Ransome's *Swallows and Amazons*, a book I read more than once: 'If not duffers, won't drown', telegraphed the father to his children, giving them permission to go sailing. I admired my father for being so like this storybook character.

On my return home for the Christmas holidays, 1930, my father told me he had become a vegetarian and explained his reasons. He had been an outstanding marksman at St Paul's School and Cambridge and a member of the Trinity College team that won the celebrated Wale Plate in 1911. When he first came to live in Matfield, it had been suggested that he should teach the village boys target shooting, and he soon had an enthusiastic group to teach once a week. He was also invited regularly by the owner of a big estate at Horsmonden to take part in pigeon and rabbit shoots.

Gradually these pursuits became unenjoyable. As a boy he had shot birds but had always felt uncomfortable when picking up a dead sparrow or pigeon. He had thought that this revulsion would pass with youth, but instead it had become so strong as to be unbearable.

Whenever he pressed the trigger, he could not help thinking of the moment of surprise when the bullet hit him in no-man's land. He had been conscious when the stretcher-bearers ran out to pick him up in December, 1914, and remembered the look of horror in their faces.

Although he gave up the shoots, he continued to teach target practice for, as he said, there was then not that bewildered look in a glazing eye to reproach him.

It was a few years before he gave up eating meat. In his boyhood, vegetarians were regarded as freaks by his parents, and it was hard to break the habit of years when he had enjoyed roast meat and even pheasants and grouse. However he knew that it was illogical to dislike killing animals and birds and yet benefit from others doing so by eating meat.

Preparing vegetarian foods was not easy for my mother. Either she or the maid had to prepare egg or fish dishes for him while the rest of the family were eating stewed meat or a joint. He liked mushrooms and would pick them in the fields near The Rosery. My mother always felt anxiety when cooking them, but she had faith in his knowledge. This confidence was stretched when he began to take an interest in edible fungi and would come in from his walks carrying scarlet and orange varieties which he requested should be cooked and served on toast. I once saw my mother, eating a spoonful from the saucepan, heroically bent on poisoning herself rather than him! No-one who knew

126

her would have been surprised, for it was always clear that her own life was less valuable to her than his.

My father had at last completed his war novel on which he had been working for some time. His impatience to get it finished had been such that, when it was half way through, he had asked my mother to write from his dictation. When he wrote he often had to stop to look up the correct spelling of a word or would even leave words out. This was due to aphasia, a loss of speech caused by brain injury, the result of the head wound from which he still had not completely recovered. My mother wrote quickly, but as the work proceeded she had come to hate the drudgery. All the frustrations a writer experiences were exploded on her head, and, although no-one was more patient, she was often in tears. My father would beg for her forgiveness for he loved her dearly; but because he was so sure of her love and loyalty he bullied her.

When the manuscript was typed, he sent a copy to a popular author who had been a comrade in France. A few weeks dragged by and the manuscript was returned with severe criticisms. Sorrowfully, my father looked at it. Whole pages, chunks, slashed with his pencil. 'Trite', 'false', 'cliche', 'my God, no' appeared thickly in the margins.

When my father had overcome his disappointment, he realised that his friend had gone to great trouble to make constructive criticism and, after a few days, commenced re-writing the faulty sections of the book. At last it was completed, bundled up and posted, by registered mail, to a publisher recommended by the friendly author.

A few weeks passed and then one morning the postman rang The Rosery bell. My father hurried to the front door to receive a neat parcel with the publishers label on it. His manuscript had been returned.

Feeling the weakness of anticipated disappointment, and hardly able to stand, my father took the parcel, remarking on the sharp frost.

'Five o'clock every morning, but you get used to it except when its bad weather, when it ain't no catch,' replied Mr Johnson.

127

'I'm glad it's not me', mustered my father, finding it difficult to conceal his disappointment.

'You wouldn't mind it if it weren't for what the War had done to you', said Mr Johnson, swinging his heavy bag over his shoulder and picking up his bicycle which he had leaned against the porch.

My father shut the door and took the parcel into the dining room. The possibility that the manuscript had been returned for alterations crossed his mind. He pulled out the typewritten letter. Only thanks, regrets. No further hope. My mother came in:

'What do they say?' she asked eagerly.

'Na poo,' he said, uttering a phrase more common in his schooldays.

'They can't have read it! You must send it to someone else. And if you don't, I shall.'

This she did, but it was again returned. War novels were not wanted. The market for them had dried up. In the 1920's people wanted to forget grief and war and the loss of loved ones. The world was hustling; new inventions, new life, jazz, and romantic lyrics had replaced 'Good-bye Tipperary'. The soldiers of the Queen and of the King, too, had been disbanded, and many of them were unemployed.

Shortly after this sad episode, my father and mother went to stay with his old school friend, Geoffrey Colbourne, and when they returned, my father started to write short stories. Geoffrey had convinced him that his talent for writing would be more successful in this form. 'The market for short stories is immense,' he urged, 'new magazines are starting up; there is much more scope than for longer works.'

For a year or so Wilfred continued, with courage, to write despite the postman's many rings of the doorbell and returned parcels.

My mother became adept in forestalling the postman's arrival by meeting him at the gate and slipping upstairs with the parcel while my father was getting up. The packages were either in the drawers of her beautiful bow-fronted chest of drawers (Grandmother Willett had, after all, bought some very good pieces of furniture in 1916) or at the bottom of her wardrobe. So far as I know they were never given to my father and remained hidden until she died. But, after a time, he must have realised that they had been rejected, and preferred not to talk to her about it.

My father's optimism that he could become a successful writer, like his friend Henry Williamson, was weakened by the failure to get his novel published. Literary success was to come later, but before that he had to confront a spiritual crisis.

Green Woodpecker

24 — A CRISIS OF BELIEF

The church militant — disillusionment — disarmament — brush with the Bishop — ordination — abandoning the church — reproach of the victims — failure.

As a churchwarden, Wilfred had gained considerable respect for his views in Matfield that the church should be truly militant in the cause of disarmament and brotherhood of man, between all nations. Of course, brotherhood between classes was too much, even for Matfield. Still, the Church Council in Matfield regularly sent to the Bishop of the diocese a request for a mission of disarmament and for authorisation of special prayers and intercessions. These were, of course, drafted by my father. The Bishop was usually too busy to attend to them; sometimes they were not even acknowledged. My father had probably not endeared himself to the Bishop by an incident when he came to Matfield for a confirmation:

'You should have that bird's nest down,' said the Bishop as he entered the church, pointing to a swallow's nest in the porch roof; 'they make a nasty mess.'

Before the vicar could reply, humbly agreeing that it should be done, my father, who knew the Bible well and, moreover, could never bear that any bird's nest should be disturbed, said:

'Yea, that sparrow hath found an house, and the swallow a nest for herself, where she may lay her young, even thine altars, O, Lord of Hosts.' The Bishop flushed, and walked on, his opinion of my father's reputed unorthodoxy no doubt confirmed.

My father was usually chosen by the vicar and the Matfield Church Council to be their representative at conferences, where he met many church dignitaries. Thus he was probably too close to the functioning of the church not to become disillusioned with the practice of Christianity. He would rise to his feet at such gatherings, trying to control his paralysed, trembling, lower lip and his speech, to urge that the church should organise against war, which was opposed to the teaching of Christ. That the promise of beauty and brotherhood was drowned in clotting blood, agony and filth, was typical of his utterances. Leaders of the church in every nation, he said, should combine together and issue a definite and final pronouncement against war. The people of the earth were longing for that lead. In the last war, the church said that all who went to fight were doing God's bidding. 'I went,' he said, 'because it was my duty, but now disarmament is the necessity.' That he embarrassed many, if not most, of his audiences was inevitable.

Discontented with the result of his campaigns to activate the church, to make it the church militant in the cause of ending war, my father decided he might become ordained. Without consulting my mother, whom he knew would seek to dissuade him, he wrote a request for admittance as an ordination candidate to a body set up by the church for the training of young men who had served in the War and who had been moved to devote themselves to the service of God. After some weeks, during which his enthusiasm waned as he thought of the practicalities of leaving his family to attend a theological college, and whether he could overcome his physical handicaps to perform the daily tasks of a vicar of a parish, his letter was returned through the 'dead letter' office. I learned of this episode through his writings. He never told my mother.

In growing doubt about the church's willingness to take a more active role in asserting the teachings of Christ, my father wrote to the Bishop who had confirmed him at St Paul's school. He besought him to initiate a movement of the whole church towards a closer co-operation with the people; to pronounce against war, poverty, unemployment and declare that the way of salvation lay in the furtherance of brotherly love. City churches were now empty that had once been full, he wrote. They could be filled again if only the church left off bickering on dogma and ritual and actively sought to inspire all men to act as Christ would have them.

In his sympathetic reply, the Bishop wrote urging my father to remain in the church to help to preserve it from the spiritual decay that might otherwise come upon it. The result of this letter was, paradoxically, to suggest to my father that he might leave the church, a step he had hitherto not contemplated, and clearly the very opposite result from that intended by the Bishop.

Uncertain now of the success both of his writing and his campaigns in the church, he was at a very low ebb. Always in his thoughts at this time were his friends and millions of other young men who had been killed in the War. They had sacrificed their lives so that future generations of young men would live out their normal span of life in peace. Already twelve years had passed since the end of the War, yet there was no sign that politicians were uniting their nations for the peace of the world nor that the Church was urging them to do so. His thoughts went back to Cambridge. He saw again the faces and heard the voices and the laughter of his friends, now dead, in those happy days. He believed in a future life. Would he meet them and would they reproach him for not doing more to prevent another war? 'Look at the years of life you have had,' they might say, 'a marriage, children, the beauty of the countryside; why have you deserved these joys when we perished in our youth?'

Sometimes, in his mind, he would answer these imaginary reproaches with bitter reflections on the loss of his own chosen career. In medicine he knew he would have succeeded, whereas he had failed to help his fellow men in the only other ways possible for someone with such handicaps as he had.

25 – RETURN FROM THE SEA

Depression – bereavement – caravan at Bexhill – a walk to the sands at night – the explanation years later – return to Matfield – Chairman of welfare committee – the reprimanded rector – the grateful bailiff.

During the Easter term, no longer a boarder, I was aware of my father's gloom and depression. My mother had been through several of these episodes when he was recovering from his wounds, but their passionate love for each other made him respond to her sweetness and sympathy. But now, some years later, it was different. His sense of the futility of war had grown apace, lessening his acceptance of the horror which had fallen on his generation. He loved her devotedly, but with a love no longer new, so her sympathy would sometimes irritate instead of soothing him. It was a time when he could not control his temper, once throwing various garments, including my mother's corsets, out of the window because they had been placed on his side of the bed. Then his old friend, Geoffrey Colbourne, developed a malignant growth and died, barely thirty-five.

This bereavement weakened his courage as no event had ever done. He had lost nearly all his boyhood friends in the war. Geoffrey had been at school with him, spent holidays with him. He was clever, and visits to him gave my father the intellectual stimulus he lacked in his life in Matfield.

Easter holidays came, and my parents decided to accept the offer of a friend's caravan sited on the cliff at Bexhill. It was very cold when we arrived. Snow had fallen and the chill in the caravan and the lean-to outside made us all shiver. My father lit the primus stove and, after a meal of baked beans and eggs, we went to bed, getting into sleeping bags which my mother had made, at my father's direction, from old army blankets. They were warm but scratchy. Sometime during the night I woke up, and crept silently outside. There was a full moon and it was still very cold but not snowing.

The cliff ended in a sharp slope down to the sands. I was surprised to see my mother running towards it. I picked up my coat, which had belonged to my cousin. It was warm, with a fur collar. As I reached the top of the cliff I saw my mother and father clearly at the water's edge. The sea was not rough though the tide was coming in. My parents were talking, but I couldn't hear what they were saying. She clutched his arm; after a few minutes they turned and walked back towards the cliff path.

I was disturbed. I felt troubled and aware that all was not well. I was 11 years old. If the event had happened a few years later, I might have met them on their return and anxiously asked for an explanation. I now crept back to bed in the lean-to. Comforted by the knowledge that they were now in bed in the caravan, I fell asleep.

In one of the long, revealing discussions which marked my close relationship with my father in later years, I asked him about the incident. He told me that night he had been filled with unutterable misery, of failure realised in himself, with no-one to blame, no excuse to soften the realisation: a failure in achievement both in his writing and in his Christian work. He felt he had attempted to succeed in tasks that sensible, normal people do not attempt. So he had limped rapidly along the cliff, down to the sand and, having reached the edge of the sea, considered his despair.

What was the good of knowledge, he thought, as he gazed at the night sky, of knowing Betelgeuse was forty million miles across, a red giant. Why Vega's blue light, the binary stars, the nebulae and other stellar systems? He felt his insignificance. The universe was vast; one puny individual was nothing. He could not bear to go on.

He thought he would dash into the waves, walk and walk until he was carried off his feet, swim the few strokes he could manage and sink to death in the waves.

But, he said, his family came into his mind before he lost absolute control of his thoughts.

'I thought that, if I died, my war pension would stop. There would have been nothing for you all to live on. I doubted if my father would help. I had made up my mind that I must go on living for all of you when your mother came running towards me, shouting. Because I had been through such turmoil, I was angry with her. She was too frightened of me to confess that she feared I might do away with myself. Instead she implored me to come in out of the cold in case I caught pneumonia. She was trembling, and I put my arm around her.' he went on. 'With all my brave talk, I clung to her. Only in her arms did I feel sheltered from the hard remorseless world.'

When we returned to Matfield, my father decided to go on being a churchwarden, despite his declining religious faith.

The village had just elected a welfare committee to help the poor by administering all the charitable funds in the village, on the basis of individual need instead of as hitherto discriminating between church and chapel folk or between those who were 'deserving' and those who, as Mr Pugh once put it, 'fritter away their money and then expect the parish to help them'. Mr Pugh and his cousins had been the charity administrators from whom the poor had to beseech charity for sickness or old age. Now my father was Chairman of the new Committee and had the vicar and some others on his side:

'I have found out', the elder Miss Storr proclaimed at one meeting, typical of many, 'that the Kingsmills have already paid the 15s. for the ambulance to take their Freddie to hospital. So there's no need for us to trouble about it. But I should like to bring up the case of Mrs Braddock; she's bedridden and there's no fireplace upstairs. Does Mr Willett think we could allow her a little milk?'

'Certainly', said my father, making a note, 'but the Kingsmills are very poor. The eldest son is out of work, Kingsmill himself doesn't earn more than 36s. a week, and they are on the hospital scheme, are they not? I think we should refund the 15s. Will anyone second this motion?'

There was silence. Then Mr Groomsbridge, the only villager on the committee, a gentle old man who always supported any humanitarian appeal, put up his hand.

In this way, my father earned the gratitude of the villagers. Not only was he better at argument than Mr Pugh and his relatives, but he also always knew the regulations governing charitable relief and could silence opposition to giving it.

The vicar would sometimes remonstrate with his headstrong warden:

'Surely nobody can deny that things have improved out of all consciousness in thirty years,' he said on one occasion, when my father had complained more bitterly than usual that damp in a tied cottage was the cause of little Sadie Jenkins being ill again with rheumatic fever. 'All things will right themselves in God's good time if we trust in him and pray.'

The British Legion was coming into more prominence. My father formed a branch in Matfield and was elected Secretary. Matfield was the only branch in the Tonbridge rural district, so he was often deputed to investigate applications to relieve the distress of ex-servicemen in neighbouring villages. At first, he consulted the vicar and churchwardens of these parishes, but found he did not carry the respect he had earned in Matfield:

'Really,' drawled the rector of one of them, 'these people have no thought for their soul's health, yet they come running when their bodily needs are not satisfied.'

'But this man has pneumonia,' my father replied, shaking, as he always did when frustrated. The rector looked at him with pale, querulous eyes, as if he had caught the rebuke in his tone. 'Well, well, perhaps this may show him how merciful God is to sinners. We will agree to share the expenses of a convalescent home for a fortnight.'

One result of my father's energetic interest in the poor and handicapped was that he had an offer of help in the garden from a retired farm bailiff, Mr Goodhill. Coles, who had helped to build the extension, had retired in a tantrum to his cottage a year or two earlier. My father found that to work eight hours a day in the garden, which he had been doing as well as his British Legion and welfare work, was tiring him out. He became short-tempered at home, bewildered my mother by refusing to play bridge or to take part in social activities, and had begun to have severe pain in his back and good leg.

Mr Goodhill offered to come and help him get the potatoes up and, when my father tried to pay him, refused:

'You do such a lot for us in the church and the village, though you are handicapped,' he said, 'you make us ashamed. So I think I'll give you a hand when I've got nothing else to do'.

My father was moved, although he subsequently managed to persuade Mr Goodhill to accept payment for one day's regular work a week.

As a result of Mr Goodhill's help, The Rosery soon had a magnificent vegetable garden, quite as good, if not better, than when my father had devoted so much of his time and energy to it in his early days at The Rosery. More than enough vegetables were grown to feed our family, and probably Mr Goodhill's as well. Vegetables were cheap in the country, so the saving on household spending may not have been much; but new potatoes, peas and beans seemed to taste better and different from those served at school.

Mr Goodhill enjoyed looking after the vegetable garden but I don't think he ever put a hoe into the flower beds. My father had taught himself to use tools with his left hand and had his favourite spade. As I had never known my father without his paralysed right arm and leg, I took it for granted that he could dig expertly with one hand, that he could use a canterbury hoe to earth up the potatoes and a fork to lift them. There were few, if any, gardening tasks that he didn't undertake as a result of his determination not to be beaten by his handicaps.

Mr Goodhill's regular work in the garden now gave my father time for a favourite hobby, carpentry. He worked in oak and made up his own designs on an art deco theme. Major Hoare, at Maycotts in the village, was delighted with a refectory table he made for him. He made a similar one to be used as a dressing table in my mother's bedroom; we now have it in our home, as sturdy as when he made it.

A new task for Anne and me was to be, as he called it, 'carpenter's mate'. I wish I could say we were willing, especially since we should have been filled with admiration for the obstacles he overcame to achieve his beautiful work. Alas, we were conscripts, anxious for the end of the tedium of holding pieces of wood while he measured and sawed and screwed. He was not very patient; if the screwdriver slipped and hit the small hand that held the wood, he would not tolerate any fuss or sucking of fingers. He expected his children to be as uncomplaining of physical discomfort as he was.

My father's physical strength was remarkable until he reached the late forties. Trunks of apple trees were stacked under the pear tree, delivered by Mr Carmen of Chill Mill Farm, Petteridge. These were sawn into big logs by my father, often using a two-handled saw with Anne or me pulling on the second handle. Then with iron wedges made at the village forge he would split the logs to burn on his study fire. With his left hand he lifted the big sledge hammer and bought it crashing down on the head of the wedge. Splinters flew as the wedge bit into the wood. Sometimes he split a log with one wedge, sometimes it needed two. He could control the hammer for the difficult sideways blows, and soon the logs would lie ready to be piled into the wheelbarrow and taken to the study window.

'Denis was sent to board at a boy's preparatory school at the age of 6' (p. 71).

Fishing on Friar's Lake: 'Denis . . . often caught . . . lines in the willow tree' (p. 55).

'A. H. Patterson, a Norfolk man, nature writer and skilled artist illustrated his letters with pen and ink sketches humorously depicting his life as an observer of birds and fish on the Norfolk Broads' (p. 167).

Violet Sassoon, 'wrapped in her grey squirrel fur coat', in Hatherleigh garden with her pet cat (p. 145).

Violet '. . . was very pretty' (p. 145).

Hatherleigh, the Sassoon home, from the Green.

Wilfred's convalescence at Folkestone in 1931: 'August that year was shadowed by grey skies . . . not many amusements for children . . . sitting on the beach, throwing stones in the sea' (p. 150).

Tunbridge Wells High School.

The bridesmaids at Evelyn's fashionable London wedding. Front row, left to right: Rosemary Finnis, Marjorie Willett, . . . (p. 119).

In The Rosery garden, 1928. '. . . the herbacious borders, with the canterbury bells, the lupins, the delphiniums [Wilfred] had grown so skilfully' (p. 176).

Denis with swallow. 'He shared [Wilfred's] interest in birds and natural history' (p. 170).

The caravan at Bexhill, 1931 (p. 133).

Fetching the milk from the
Pleasure Boat Inn, Hickling.

Washing up in the houseboat on Hickling Broad.
'[Wilfred] could . . . now use his left hand to do
much of the work of his useless right hand' (p. 37).

Wilfred 'punted skilfully with one hand' (p. 102).

Anne at St Clair, 1932. '. . . it was important for a small private school to show it offered good value for money . . .' (p. 179).

1916 − Thomas and Susie Willett 'had recently purchased a large Edwardian house, The Homestead, in Tunbridge Wells' (p. 25).

'. . . the last of the three children to leave The Rosery . . .' (p. 193). The author in 1946.

The Rosery in 1945. '. . . the wild profusion of overgrown shrubs' (p. 176).

St Luke's Church, Matfield, drawn by E. G. Grenham . . . 'the quiet country churchyard, with its lychgates and yew trees . . . in 1983 unchanged since my father had been churchwarden' (p. 195).

Wilfred in 1960.

26 – DEATH OF GRANDFATHER WILLETT

Grandfather ill – Susies retires to Folkestone – Wilfred votes Labour – and reads Lenin – a funeral ordeal – speculation and the will – quarrel – reconciliation.

Grandfather Willett had been suffering from a throat complaint, at first thought to be an infection. But the doctor told my grandmother that he feared it was either tubercular or malignant, and that in either case he could not long. Soon two nurses were installed and Grandmother went to Folkestone to recover, she said, from the shock and have a rest from the turmoil in the house.

My father, who had always been fond of his 'Pater', readily agreed to go to Tunbridge Wells every day to sit with him.

Grandfather was pathetically pleased to have his son there and, although he did not speak in the weeks that he was dying, often put out his hand and touched him.

It struck my father that he would have many hours in which to read. So he decided they should be used to explore his new interest in Socialism. He had, without telling anyone, voted Labour in the 1929 Election, partly because he thought their record on disarmament was better than the Conservatives' and partly because of his dismay at the growing unemployment. A few years earlier one million was thought to be the hard core beyond which the figures would not rise, but now in 1930 they were moving towards three million.

He visited his friend Mr Rayward, the bookseller at Goulden & Curry in Tunbridge Wells High Street, with whom he had often discussed politics, and asked him for books about Lenin. He bought *The Life of Lenin* and Lenin's own *Imperialism*.

My father's previous studies had included world literature, and in the years of his disablement he had read and bought many books. He still did not read as fluently or quickly as he did before his wound, and found that he needed an encyclopaedia to unravel some of the new knowledge he was anxious to acquire. Such words as social democrat, reactionary, social-chauvinism, petit bourgeoisie, Fabian and many others were unfamiliar and necessary to understand if he were to grasp the meaning of socialist and communist writings.

Watching by his father's bed, he decided that Lenin was concerned only for a happy and peaceful world and that the working class held the future in their hands. This was not anti-British, he decided: as always, a patriot. For, after all, the good sense of the British people would prefer evolution without the revolution and violence of Russia.

After four weeks Grandfather died. Grandmother had returned from Folkestone some days previously and shed some tears for the husband who had always been kind and good to her, had always allowed her to run both their lives, and whom, perhaps, she had loved when they both young.

It happened on the day of Grandfather's funeral that the weather was bad, and so, instead of playing games, the school was sent out for a walk. The crocodile of girls was walking two by two at a brisk pace along the pavement, the mistress on duty bringing up the rear, when a funeral cortege came slowly along the road leading to the cemetry, and passed us. Tears ran out of my eyes. The girl walking by my side noticed and asked what had happened. As I breathed, 'Grandfather's funeral!' she turned and whispered over her shoulder. There was a buzz along the line and sympathetic eyes were turned towards me. The mistress came up, took my hand, and led me back to walk with her. To be the centre of attention was pleasing, but the truth was that my distress was not for my grandfather but for the shock of seeing my brother Denis, his white face turned towards me as he sat in front of the first funeral car. The memory of his face haunted me. I wondered why my parents had agreed that such a sensitive boy should be submitted to this ordeal. It seemed that Grandmother had insisted on it.

My father had been made senior trustee, partly because Uncle Lewis was younger but also because Grandfather had considered that Lewis had the cares of Fleet Street on his shoulders, whereas Wilfred would be free to comfort and advise his mother.

140

Unfortunately, as my father had always suspected, Grandfather had occupied himself with speculation: the safe was found to be full of worthless shares, some £20,000 to £30,000 of capital having been dissipated in this way. Grandmother's distress was inconsolable. She would have to give up the Homestead and move to a smaller house. Other economies would have to be made, and among these she proposed reducing my father's allowance.

'Bloody Hell,' said my father.

'Wilfred!'

'I'm sorry, Mater, but really it's unfair to expect me to manage all the expenses of the family on my pension and what little I can earn by writing. After all,' he added, incautiously, 'perhaps Pater wouldn't have lost all that money if he hadn't had to speculate because you were spending more than his income!'

A stormy scene followed, which ended with Grandmother Susie saying she was too upset to want to see him for a time: all communications had better be conducted through the solicitor until she felt stronger and more able to stand his unkindness towards his bereaved mother.

When my father discussed the quarrel with my mother in the calm of his study at The Rosery, she soothed him with her commonsense:

'It's just as well,' she said, 'that you won't have to go running into Tunbridge Wells every day. These last two months have tired you out. And, anyway, I am sure she has no intention of stopping the allowance; she just wanted to make you feel grateful that she was prepared to make a sacrifice for you. Don't be too hard on her,' she added. 'After all, you should remember that she has just lost your father, and she will have to make some changes in the way she lives.'

It was a full six months before a stiff little note arrived inviting Wilfred and Eileen to have lunch at Derwent Lodge, Grandmother's new home. Meanwhile the allowance had been continued as before.

The initial coolness of their reception over, Grandmother was soon telling them how well settled she was in her new home. Dora and the cook had been pleased to stay in her service and

141

she had decided to keep the car, for the time being. 'There are shops, of course, quite close,' she said, 'but this is not such a good end of the town as The Homestead. Also Lady Bull has urged me to take up bridge again and I have given one or two little afternoon bridge parties. No evening parties of course. I feel it's too soon. . . .'

It was not long before the family were also invited to lunch at Derwent Lodge. To me it seemed as if Grandmother had brought the Homestead with her. The carpet in the hall and on the stairs was red, as that in the Homestead had been. The drawing room looked exactly the same, not even smaller for Grandmother had had two rooms knocked into one. General Wolfe was dying on the stairs. When we went into lunch, Venice was hanging on the wall behind Grandmother's chair, exactly as it had at the Homestead.

An interesting feature of Derwent Lodge was the lavatory, a small room halfway up the first flight of stairs and convenient for anyone in too much of a hurry to reach the bathroom on the first floor. The 'half-way lavatory' had a splendid polished mahogany throne and a charmingly-patterned china bowl. Grandmother had had partial central-heating installed, a novelty at this time, and there was a radiator in the lavatory. She had not, however, copied my father's notion of placing a bookcase in the only lavatory in The Rosery. Frenzied shouts 'Come out! You're reading!' outside the locked door were the inevitable results of such literary thoughtfulness.

27 — MATFIELD, 1931

Percy — Ebenezer — East End hoppers — brush with village doctor — the Sassoons.

There were more cars on the roads of Matfield now, but Miss Selina and Miss Eleanor Storr still rode their bicycles, old-fashioned now, and Bernard Pursglove, Miss Reeves' errand boy, still pedalled his big bike with the iron basket in front, full of groceries. Sometimes I heard my mother on the telephone ordering a packet of 'medium-size drapery', which I learned was the recognised code name for sanitary towels. Percy Butler still wheeled his cart with bundles of woodshavings called chips, for lighting fires in winter, from house to house, and waited outside the Grange at 'break' for boys to throw him biscuits over the wall. He always wore an ancient 'morning' coat.

Percy's ragged clothes, toothless mouth, matted hair and simple mind made him an object of derision but also of fear. I think the Rosery children and the Grange boys half believed him to be a kind of hobgoblin. Children in the village made a sport of jumping out at him behind a hedge and running away in terror that was not altogether pretence when he flailed his arms and shouted at them. When his old mother died and there was no-one to look after him in the cottage in Chapel Row, he was taken to the asylum at Barming. 'Barmy' was the local name for lunacy, and is since then used more widely, but Percy was not mad; he had just never grown up.

Small changes there had been. There was now a parish hall beside the Wheelwright Arms. Matfield had acquired a fire station. Mr Hubbard of Matfield Place had created a garage for the fire engine out of one of his cottages alongside the pond. The crew — shopkeepers, farm labourers and Mr Hubbard's own chauffeur, Wilfred Carter — were summoned by siren.

The old Ebenezer chapel remained for a few more years until it was bulldozed and council houses erected close by. Miss

Reeves donated a piece of land in front of her shop for a new chapel, which was to rise proudly, in 1937, built of red brick and three times the size of the old. The elders of the chapel decided to leave the old graveyard, although removing the yew trees. Zippor Buggs still rests in peace.

Matfield was only a few miles from the main hop area in Kent: Paddock Wood, Beltring, Wateringbury, Horsmonden and Goudhurst. All the pubs in Matfield had signs 'No hoppers served' in September when families came from the East End of London to pick the hops, garnering them into huge bath-like bins and being paid as piece workers. For many East Enders this was their annual holiday, but the huts they were housed in were primitive. Sanitary arrangements were almost non-existent: frequently there were outbreaks of scarlet fever and diptheria among the children. Country people did not like the hoppers, and they were not welcomed in shops or pubs. It was thought they might harbour fleas; village people would not sit by them on the buses. They looked very poor. The children sometimes had no shoes. If, as the villagers suspected, they stole fruit from gardens, this seemed to be their only crime. There were sometimes fights in the camps, but no violence or robbery that I can remember was ever reported in Matfield.

Because of his medical background, my father was concerned that the village people in Matfield should be well looked after when ill. He would insist that the Charity Committee paid for extra milk for pregnant mothers if their incomes were low, and he had many tussles with the village doctor, never hesitating to complain if he fell short of my father's high standards.

The doctor was a kindly man but indolent, certainly not fond of turning out at night or on Sundays. Thus he made a bad mistake over the treatment of Bobbie Fletcher, who fell off a wall one Sunday morning. Bobbie's mother called round to see the doctor, but he said Bobbie ought to be in church not climbing walls; if the arm still hurt, he would see him in surgery the following day.

My father called at the house a week or two later to give Mrs Fletcher a chit for free milk, since she was expecting another baby, and asked why Bobbie was not at school.

'His arm is still bad', replied Mrs Fletcher, 'It's his right arm too and he doesn't seem as if he can straighten it'.

My father made a rapid diagnosis that Bobbie's arm would most probably never fully mend. This was a serious matter for an agricultural family, for it meant that Bobbie would not get a job on a farm when he left school. He told Mrs Fletcher he would arrange for Bobbie to see a consultant in London. It says much for our village doctor's good temper, if not for his medical skill, that he never complained about my father's high-handed behaviour towards one of his patients and continued to treat our family free of charge. But Bobbie's arm didn't mend, despite the consultant, and there was much bad feeling in the village about it.

For a time after Mrs Gill's death, my mother had had no close woman friend, or confidante, in the village. This gap was filled most happily by Violet Sassoon, the wife of Michael, a brother of Siegfried, the widely-acclaimed poet.

The Sassoons lived at Hatherleigh on the Green, which they rented from the married daughter of a former vicar of Matfield. Violet was middle-aged and, in spite of being short and stout, was very pretty. She had bright blue eyes and a soft pink and white skin. She always wore a coat, even in the house. They were of silk or chiffon and seemed to float around her. Her outstanding attraction was the warmth of her personality. I sometimes called, leaning my bicycle against the old brick wall, and sure of a welcome. She taught me to play mahjong and if it was a fine day in summer, would tell me to get out the croquet mallets. I spent much time fetching the balls from the flower bed, for she loved a joke and cannoning the balls off the court amused us both.

Violet provided the gaiety which my mother's life lacked. The serious business of making ends meet and anxiety, which never lifted, over my father's health had submerged a delightful sense of humour, quite different from his, so sharp and ironical. Now she and Violet would spend hours together in intimate conversation with much laughter.

Michael was an engineer. He was apprenticed when he left school, about 1907, to the Thornycroft Works at Basingstoke.

His mother was a Thornycroft and still lived in Weirleigh, a gloomy house, resembling a fortress on the road between Matfield and Paddock Wood. After studying engineering at Clare College, Cambridge, he married Violet and went to live at Shoreham-on-Sea, working for Sir Henry Ricardo, where he helped to produce a car called the Dolphin. Then, with Violet and their baby son Leo, he emigrated to Canada where he started an auto radiator repair shop — anti-freeze had still not been invented. A year or two later he moved 200 miles north with the family to take charge of the machinery at a salmon-canning factory.

When he returned to England with his wife and two sons (a third, Hamo, was born in 1920) he acquired a pilot's licence and for a short time owned Jean Batten's Gypsy Moth, in which she had flown to New Zealand in 1936. The Sassoons were much better off than my parents, for in 1927 an aunt died and left enough money for Michael to live comfortably. He occupied himself by doing up old cars in the garden of Hatherleigh, until later, in the 'thirties, he started a business with William Godfrey in agricultural machinery in the nearby village of Brenchley which continues to this day.

Violet was devoted to animals. A huge Persian cat always slept in the best armchair. She was vigilant against the neglect or ill-treatment of any cat in Matfield or Brenchley. One of her habits was to feed the ducks on the pond at midnight. She would walk to the pond, wrapped in her grey squirrel fur coat, calling 'dickie-duck, dickie-duck' and throw scraps of bread into the pond for her pets. I do not remember that this nocturnal excursion was thought eccentric.

My father liked Michael and his eldest son, Leo, who was at Cambridge. Both of them would call at The Rosery and spend many hours conversing about politics, often arguing but always with the utmost good humour.

28 – SADNESS AND TROUBLE

Homosexual assault – escape into Little Women *– self-diagnosis – sacrifice of teeth – perilous boat-trip at Folkestone – Grandmother Susie's tenderness – bridge for Kent.*

Since his birth in 1918 my brother, Denis, had been an idolised child. Now, thirteen years later in 1931, a blow fell which, but for my parents' courage, resolution and love for each other, would have crushed them more thoroughly even than my father's war wound and its aftermath.

Denis, a charming, fair-haired, intelligent child was the victim of a savage homosexual assault by a teacher. My parents fortunately could not look into the future and see that the shock would profoundly and adversely affect his future life.

He was required to give evidence against the criminal in Court: more stress. Perhaps psychological treatment, which was not suggested, would have helped Denis, but more likely it would have made no difference. I believe that he never recovered from the damage, that he never regained self-confidence and that he was ever afterwards mistrustful of people and even of life itself. Perhaps only a family with a tragedy like my brother's can be spared criticism for the 'illiberal' belief that known practising homosexuals should not be allowed to teach in schools. In my brother's case, the man's proclivity was not known, for private schools were as vigilant as they could be to protect their pupils and their reputations from damage.

Barely two years separated us in age, and although I saw him only in the holidays, my memories of our early childhood are pleasant. Most of all I remember the Christmases, gathering holly from the trees in the garden together, and hanging it in the house, watching for the postman coming up the road on his bicycle, pooling what little money we had for presents. Suddenly I lost this friendly brother. Suddenly he became quiet and withdrawn, pale and thin.

147

I was, of course, aware that some terrible calamity had happened. Denis was home but it was not the holidays. My mother and father talked in quiet voices, fell silent if I entered the room. Strangers came and went, once even a policeman in uniform. At last I asked my mother what had happened:

Almost casually, she said: 'There are men who go to other men rather to a woman. Sometimes they interfere with boys' privacy'. As an explanation it was bewildering, but I asked no more questions.

At this time I was very happy at St Clair. The work was easy and I won my father's praise. Now it seemed he had little time for me. I retreated into a world created by reading. I had read all G. A. Henty's books from *By Conduct and Courage* to *By Sheer Pluck* and had developed a liking for mournful and moralistic Victorian books. Mrs Montgomery's *Misunderstood*, Louisa M. Alcott's *Little Women* with the tragic death of Beth, *Eric, or Little by Little*: all these seemed in keeping with the sadness I felt around me. My mother cried a lot these days. And my own tears dropped onto the pages of books, but the insubstantial emotion vanished like a cobweb.

My father became ill. He was racked with pain in his back and limbs, and at night I could hear him groaning. The doctor came and diagnosed rheumatism brought about by occasional sleeping in a tent in the garden and not wearing enough clothes. This theory my father dismissed. He had very little faith in our local doctor and told my mother to make an appointment with the dentist in Tunbridge Wells to take out all his teeth. As often before, he diagnosed himself. He felt sure that the pain and weakness in his limbs came from a sceptic source, and he judged it was most likely to be teeth. Despite my mother's protests he was driven into Tunbridge Wells and had all his teeth removed. His physical courage accepted the drastic action indicated by his self-confident diagnosis, as it had done in 1915 when he may have saved his life.

But this time his self-diagnosis was wrong. The pain grew no better, and to this disappointment was added the discomfort of his new teeth. He decided to make an appointment to see the neurologist at the London Hospital who had been a fellow student, now well on his way to fame. My father had been a better student than he, but the contrast between my father's shattered health and career and his friend's good fortune affected my father far less than it did him. He went to great trouble with his examinations; at last he pronounced that recovery would be complete but slow. There must be no walking and much rest.

Relieved though my mother was, she told the consultant that my father was always attempting activities that would tire even a normal man out. Perhaps if he had taken more care of himself the illness would not have happened.

'I must tell you, Mrs Willett,' replied the neurologist, 'that if Wilfred hadn't this strong will and drive he would never have been anything but an invalid since he was wounded. But now he must rest for three months.'

Grandmother Willett, who had paid one visit to The Rosery bearing grapes and sick-room advice, was informed that the specialist had prescribed three month's complete rest for my father. Without consulting my mother, she had herself driven to Folkestone where her brother Great Uncle Frank Seager lived. Great Uncle Frankie, a genial and elderly bachelor, was an estate agent. At his sister's request he arranged to rent a large flat over shops in the High Street for the month of August.

The proposal to spend August in Folkestone was acceptable to my parents. Not only would my father obey instructions to lie-up better when he had no garden to harass him by seeing work that needed to be done. But Denis by now was obviously a very unhappy boy. He had been accepted at Cranbrook School, an old grammar-foundation independent school, for the Autumn term. My mother had an almost mystical belief in the value of sea air. She thought it would cure Denis's unhappiness before starting the new school, as well as my father's rheumatism.

As far I knew, the relatives were either unaware of the court case pending over Denis's assailant or they preferred not to talk about it. Newspapers were much less salacious than now. I do not remember hearing that the case had been reported. Almost certainly I would have seen a newspaper in the house had any-thing come out. Probably the only people, including relatives, my parents ever discussed it with were Violet and Michael Sassoon.

But silence didn't help.

Folkestone in August that year was shadowed by grey skies, and cold winds blew incessantly. The flat was on the second floor, which meant my father had to spend much time lying on the sofa so as not to use the stairs more than once a day. My mother, of course, stayed with him reading the books we found at his request at the many second-hand bookshops in the town.

Folkestone was not at that time a resort with many amusements for children, particularly if they had little pocket-money. We used to enjoy taking the big lift or cable car from the Leas down to the beach, but it was pebbled and sloping sharply. Sometimes I would swim in the rough sea but this meant leaving my sister on the beach and she cried at being left alone. My brother, too, was an anxiety to me.

We had been in Folkestone a few days when my mother exhorted me not to leave Denis alone. 'When you're out together, don't let him go off alone,' she said. 'I want you always to stay with him.'

Not surprisingly, Denis, who became more morose than I ever remembered, rebelled sharply at the watch-dog system, which he soon discovered. If we were sitting on the beach throwing stones in the sea he would suddenly get up and hurry back to the promenade. It was August, so there were many people walking up and down. Try as I would, running along with pebbles in my sand shoes that I had had no time to remove, I often lost him. To make matters worse, my sister Anne, then about seven, to whom he was much kinder than he was to me, developed a gumboil which kept her at home for a week in considerable pain.

I was not happy; uncertain about precisely what it was that I was supposed to be protecting Denis against. I felt that the more I tried to look after him, the more he tormented me by disappearing. As I think about it now, he was much more to be pitied than I. He must have felt that he was no longer trusted, that he was somehow to blame for the dreadful thing that had happened two months earlier, or, worse, that his parents shared his fears of another shameful event.

Uncle Frankie, who was very unlike his sister Susie Willett, having a soft, kindly nature, realised that the children were having a dull time and arranged a boat trip for us. He told us to meet him at the harbour at three o'clock one afternoon. Once there, he introduced us to an old boatman, who, he said, was a friend of his and would take us all out in his large rowing boat.

All three of us had qualms as we settled ourselves in the boat, Uncle Frankie at the tiller with Anne sitting beside him. We were well accustomed to boats and the water, having spent many holidays on the Norfolk Broads, but we had never been out on the sea, except on a large steamer at Eastbourne.

As we emerged on the other side of the harbour wall it was to a very rough sea. The boat bounced up and down between the huge waves and the boatsman was clearly having a struggle to keep the boat moving. Uncle Frankie smiled benignly round at us all, delighted that he had been able to give us such a treat. It wasn't long before Denis's greenish colour changed to white and he was violently sick over the side of the boat. Anne had buried her face in Uncle Frankie's jacket and was therefore unaware of the colossal walls of water, so it seemed to me, sweeping towards us.

'Don't you think we ought to turn back Uncle Frankie?' I quavered at last, 'Denis seems to be rather sick.'

'Best thing possible to get his sea legs,' Uncle Frankie replied, cheerfully. 'Never sea-sick more than once you know, and he has been looking peeky lately. Fresh sea air will do him a world of good.'

As I gritted my teeth, and thought that we should all soon be clinging to an upturned boat, the boatman himself decided that he had had enough of the very hard work, and we were landed at the jetty, Uncle Frankie still very pleased with himself. As he told my parents: The girls had thoroughly enjoyed it, but Denis had been a bit off-colour.

The month went by very slowly, but my father's health was improving. Soon he could get up and down the stairs without trouble. My mother no longer had to read to him at night when he could not sleep for the pain.

It was time to return to The Rosery. My Grandmother Willett had paid for the holiday, and it may be that this summer marked the softening of her relationship with my father and his family. There were no more estrangements. Although she did not come to The Rosery often, my parents often played bridge with her at Derwent Lodge and she sometimes asked the whole family to lunch. She and my mother tolerated each other better over the bridge table than elsewhere, for my mother was a precise and talented player who was later chosen to play for Kent in county championships.

She was humble about this achievement, always asserting that Wilfred was a good player and could have been even better if he had cared to spend as much time on the game as she did. Bridge players could become obsessive, especially in a town like Tunbridge Wells, where she often played, and where servants still made it possible for their mistresses to spend long hours at the bridge table. My mother played because she enjoyed it, but Wilfred's requirements to be taken here or there always had priority.

One of my father's first actions on returning from a holiday was to walk to his beloved hut. The Rosery garden was wedge-shaped; the house stood in its widest part and the hut at the other end where the garden seemed to vanish into the surrounding fields. My father had made a writing table and chair and a narrow bed for the hut and had built a verandah onto it. There stood his bird-watching binoculars on a stand. There was no noise except for the singing of the birds, the distant hum of a tractor and the wind or the rain. In summer the adjoining fields were white with marguerites, growing wild in the tall grass, and in spring the little wood was a sea of bluebells.

29 — IDEOLOGIES

The churchwarden militant — Lenin's new economic system to abolish war — a tiger by the tail — the vicar's admiration — Eileen and socialism — Wilfred's new friends — Eileen's charm.

The new term had begun. Denis took the bus daily to Cranbrook and Anne and I travelled in the other direction to Tunbridge Wells.

My father had now sufficiently recovered from his illness to write in his hut in the morning, continuing the text for *British Birds* which Roland Green had agreed to illustrate. He worked regularly in the garden for an hour or two in the afternoon, but thinking about the church most of the time.

He felt strangely without hope, living in a kind of philosophic hand-to-mouth existence, not knowing from day to day what should be his religious or political faith. He still believed in God, but had very little trust in the church and its doctrines. Yet he clung to the humanity of Christ's message in order to preserve himself in the old tradition. He thought perhaps that G. K. Chesterton was right in saying that when men assert Christianity has failed, the truth is that it has been found difficult and therefore has not been tried.

He thought sadly that he had spent ten years urging the church to give a dynamic lead in bringing about a Disarmament Treaty so that there would be no more war and in nurturing closer accord between classes in England, yet all that had happened was that the church's dogmas and teaching had perpetuated outworn myths which had retarded man's progress towards happiness and freedom.

However, he still wished to retain his post as churchwarden. He reasoned that this was not dishonest since he acknowledged the spiritual truth of Christianity. Moreover, practically, as a churchwarden, it was possible to do things for the poor in Matfield through the Charity Committee. He did not trust others on the Committee to be as liberal and understanding of the poor as he was. In this assessment he was not mistaken, for the church ladies had not mellowed with the years and their judgement of morals was more intertwined with the granting of charity than ever.

The vicar had called several times during his illness and now called again at teatime. My father rang the bell and Frances, who had replaced Clara and Mrs Cheesman, brought in the silver teatray, now with a number of dents.

'Well, Willett,' said the vicar, cheerily (he retained the old-fashioned tradition of using surnames), 'I am glad to see you up and about again and so will all of us at church.'

.My father responded politely. For a time the talk centred on church matters, collections, Armistice Day service, guest clerics and so on.

Emboldened by the friendly atmosphere as the vicar sipped his second cup of tea, my father launched into an attack on armaments, although well aware the vicar hating anything akin to politics:

'I think it's frightful to grow rich by buying shares in companies that make arms,' said my father, 'I understand that the Bishop won't answer a request for special prayers for the Disarmament Conference because he is staying with a baronet who made a fortune out of arms in the last war.'

My father had raised his voice and the vicar, no doubt thinking that to provoke an argument would retard his recovery, replied calmly:

'Yes, these things are not easy to follow, for we do not know all that lies behind. But, when it comes to particular individuals, it is not for us to judge. That is for God who knows all, and we should be careful lest we condemn our fellow Christians.'

My father was aware that, in the gentlest way, he had been rebuked. Yet he never found it easy to give way on any matter on which he held strong views. He was certainly the very embodiment of 'the church militant'. The vicar must have reflected yet again, as often before, that in his churchwarden he had a tiger by the tail.

'I have been reading some newspaper articles about Lenin,'

went on my father, unabashed and eagerly. 'Some of the things he is reported as saying seem to make sense. He said that the Versailles Treaty would not abolish war, that the only thing that will do so is an international economic system. I have wondered if God is showing us the way to rid ourselves of war through the medium of Lenin's discovery.'

Not surprisingly, this was too much for the vicar:

'God forbid you should think that of the man who was the means of sending tens of thousands of Christians to horrible deaths in an attempt to kill all religion, in whose country parents may not now teach God's love to their children. No, no, Willett, my dear man. Don't think of it. You have been carried away in your eagerness to find quick solutions to these grievous problems. Yet, rest assured God will provide his own solution when men are fit to receive it.'

So saying, the vicar rose to leave, pressing my father's hand warmly to show that his affection for him was as ever. Indeed he was a true friend: in spite of his prosy ways he knew that my father's outbursts were an expression of frustration that he could not single-handedly make men into the saints he would have them be. Moreover, the vicar, as he once told my mother, admired my father more than any man he knew for the service he gave so unstintingly to the poor and the disabled, and for his determination to serve the primary purpose in life — to spare other generations of men the sufferings of his own.

Yet he could only answer in platitudes when my father said the church had a duty to explain why God had allowed 50 million to be killed or grieviously wounded in a war in which both sides thought the same Christian God was helping them.

And when my father once told him, 'I don't consider I was wounded and my life work ruined by an individual German, before I had a chance to do any good, but because man had neglected the teaching of Christ'. Then the vicar could only shake his head and say:

'The church must leave politics alone. Whenever she goes off her sphere and tries to meddle with politics she becomes reft with dissension in her own ranks.'

My mother took my father to task for not being more cheerful now that he was feeling better, Denis had been settled at a new school and, although money difficulties were never far away, at least there was not a pressing crisis in their daily lives.

'You look so miserable sometimes; I wish you wouldn't when you can look so charming. Katie Castle said this morning what a wonderful smile you had and how kind you are to everyone.'

'I can't help thinking out problems and ideas sometimes,' he replied, flattered in spite of himself.

'I can't see what good it does worrying yourself to death over these things you can't alter,' she said. Her view was that governments always made muddles but it was no use trying to do anything about it. Life was a perpetual struggle to meet bills. Yet, relatively poor though we were by the standards of the gentry, she was unfailingly kind to people in distress; she always gave away our outgrown clothes, even those of sentimental value like baby dresses and shawls. She always explained, ever tender of the feelings of the real poor, that these were garments she had herself received as outgrown by her nieces.

My mother's lack of enthusiasm for Christianity and the church had disappointed my father in their early years. Now he knew her too well to suppose he could kindle an interest in socialism. He asked her to read aloud to him from some of Lenin's writings and, although she did so, she was disinclined for any discussion. He knew that she was apprehensive about his new philosophy not because it was alien to nearly everyone in Matfield, especially their friends, but because it might result in stress which could impair his health. This was always her paramount consideration.

She had an obstinate honesty. Even to please him, she could not pretend to share his ideological and idealistic goals. She was not an intellectual; the pursuit of philosophic ideas did not draw her as it did him. She hoped that, by providing him with the comfort of selfless love, she could do more for him than by joining in a cause, which she would not do because she did not believe in it.

She was not conventional; the unorthodoxy of my father's views in an English village in the thirties she was able to absorb because everyone except him was relatively unimportant to her and their criticisms, therefore, were like pinpricks. Of course, she liked, even loved, many people, but he was the giant in her life.

Although she did not realise it at the time, his new political beliefs were the biggest strain their mutual love had ever borne. That it was surmounted was a triumph when some predicted a disaster. But those who did were people who did not know them well, who did not realise that he depended on her and trusted her beyond the bounds of an ordinary relationship. Without really trying, she was able to charm and please most of his new left-inclined friends, who included Palme Dutt, the Indian communist. He loved her for it. As for her, it was not likely that she would retreat from her life's work of loving Wilfred.

30 – POLITICAL ARGUMENTS

Civil war in Ireland – unemployment – socialism – National Government – the League of Nations and disarmament – Eileen protests – Communist Party – National Union of Agricultural Workers – Harry Pearson.

Since 1918 every political development had been closely followed by my father, always with the hope that Baldwin or MacDonald or the Coalition governments would seek better understanding between nations. The civil war in Ireland, which did not end until 1923, worried him. Yet at that time he agreed with most of the dinner party conversations in Matfield, and at The Homestead, which all followed the same line: the Sinn Feiners were making their country into a sorry mess with lawlessness and murder. The Irish constabulary, supported by the courageous 'Black and Tans', were gradually bringing peace and order there.

'Nobody,' said Grandmother Willett at dinner, 'could understand the Irish or what they wanted. The best thing for solving the Irish problem was to shut Ireland off from any outside communication; at the end of six months the problem would have settled itself as all the Irish would have murdered each other!'

On unemployment, my father never accepted the conventional view of his class and times, that it was a pity so much taxation had to be levied to pay these wasters. My father knew, from the many working-class homes he entered to distribute charity or to encourage and help those who were disabled in the war or in agricultural accidents, that unemployment in the family was an evil to be dreaded: skilled men would walk many miles in the hope of securing work.

He found it difficult to understand why, when millions of men had been killed in the War, there should not be enough work for those who survived. In this misunderstanding as in much of

158

Marxist doctrine, he allowed his warm and generous feelings, his pity for the unfortunate, his outsize sense of fair play to distort his judgement and blind his exceptional intelligence.

One of the businessmen who had come to live in Matfield lately was more than commonly clever, and my father found this Mr Burman a congenial companion, more knowledgeable about public affairs than others in Matfield, although with unconventional if not idiosyncratic opinions.

'Yes, unemployment is a terrible problem', said Mr Burman, puffing his cigar, in one cosy after-dinner discussion. 'I think the ultimate solution will have to be found in some sort of conscription for public work, though how it will be managed don't ask me'. He shrugged his shoulders as though thankful it was not his concern. 'That cigar drawing all right? If not, throw it away and take another.'

My father was unwilling to let the subject drop and anxious to introduce some of his recently discovered socialist theories:

'You would agree, sir', he said deferentially (he was then 39 and Mr Burman was a much older man), 'that this is an age of discoveries, the atom, protons, the electrons, wireless, relativity, vitamins. So why not in systems of government? Socialism means sharing things equally by law after a long period of adjustment and the church must be revivified and become again a power for good'.

'Ha, ha, Willett. You want to make things hum,' replied Mr Burman, good-humouredly. 'The trouble is that to start men producing things to sell you have to get enough people to hazard their money and, naturally, you must give them a chance of a fair return. The worker loses nothing if the concern goes bust. Also we have to find markets, and that's none too easy these days with every nation producing our kinds of goods, and some cheaper than us'.

The National Government of 1931 was welcomed by my father. Although he was reading more and more political works — Marx, Engels, Lenin — he was deeply dismayed by the economic crisis of 1931 and the world slump. England had a deficit of more than a hundred million pounds. The getting-together of all three Parties, in government, or at least leaders in all three, to save England was an effort in national salvation of which he thoroughly approved.

But, above all, he wanted to see something done to abolish war with absolute certainty. The more he read, the more he was convinced that the only solution would be international socialism, achieved in England, of course, through peaceful evolution. Never, at any time, did my father want to see England rent with civil strife, nor indeed losing her national identity. But the League of Nations had failed to achieve a Disarmament Treaty, and he believed this failure would make another war inevitable, something he could not bear to contemplate for younger people, including his own children, growing up in England.

Efforts to convince some of his friends in Matfield that Lenin had found the answer to end war were unsuccessful.

He strolled in one evening to see Mr Punnett and allowed him to explain the Lorrette system of pruning which my father knew rather more than he, having applied the system to his own fruit trees for years. When the explanation was finished, and Mr Punnett asked him to walk round the garden, it seemed to be a good time for plunging into his new theories:

'Do you know that Lenin has found the cause of war and has proved up to the hilt that it is capitalism and the necessity to find markets and export capital that drives nations eventually into war?'

Mr Punnett halted in his tracks, as if he had been shot.

'My dear fellow, whoever have you been listening to? Really, you shouldn't be taken in by what these socialist agitators put out. Industry is the life and breath to a country like ours. All these socialists do is to stir up trouble, unsettling God-fearing honest workers.'

'Oh, no,' remonstrated my father, anxious at this point not to be taken for a 'Bolshie' or a 'Red'. 'Obviously much of what he says wouldn't be applicable to England. Still, the man's a genius and thoroughly well read. Do you know he had read Shakespeare and Dickens and was familiar with many of the world's classical writings?'

'Well, all I can say is if he was well educated, it's a pity he

160

didn't die of brain fever instead of living to ruin Russia body and soul!'

Soon, it was all round Matfield that my father had 'gone over' to the socialists. My mother was discomforted when several of her friends said they couldn't understand how a man who had given so much for his country could favour a system that had caused so much misery in Russia. 'Does he want us to lose all our money?' asked Mrs Hogg, our next-door neighbour, whose husband was a financial expert known in the city as 'the company doctor'.

My mother spoke to my father about it. 'I hate it when people talk about you like that,' she said, repeated Mrs Hogg's words. 'Everybody knows you would do anything to help anyone, but don't you think you are going too far in this? I don't think its quite fair on the children or me. I don't want you to change your beliefs, but you needn't make all the village and our friends think you've gone quite mad!'

My mother had thoroughly worked herself up, mainly because she was worried that too much opposition and argument would be bad for him. Never far from her thoughts at such times was the medical advice she had received when he left hospital that intense excitement should be avoided in case it brought on the traumatic epilepsy caused by his brain injury. He had not had an attack for more than sixteen years since 1915. Yet she was always apprehensive; sometimes, as now, she would use his concern for the children to try to stop him doing something she considered a risk to his health.

But as she feared, my father was furious. Here was he trying to make people understand that there could not be lasting peace unless the economic system was altered, and all that happened was that people thought he was a crank, made unstable by his wound.

In a fine frenzy he accused my mother of leading an aimless existence, indifferent to the suffering caused by the war. Even as he said it, he knew this was not true.

He banged out of the house and limped off to the woods, returning after a period of reflection to tell my mother that, although he was truly sorry he had upset her, he could not and

161

would not cease to work for a world in which their children and the children of others could live in peace.

Some days later, without telling my mother, he went to London and joined the Communist Party. To his surprise it was over an hour before he could persuade the party official to enrol him. Apparently he could not believe my father was in earnest and could be of any use. Several things my father said must have struck him as both impractical and condescending.

By about this time my father was becoming known for his writing. Besides numerous articles in ornithological journals, he had written a much-praised book, *British Birds*. So not surprisingly, the initial reluctance to accept the new recruit turned to enthusiasm. My father was soon in communication with Party leaders. Harry Pollitt paid us a visit at The Rosery and had a long talk with him in the study. Whether as a result of this, or not, my father organised a local branch of the National Union of Agricultural Workers. This initiative was very unpopular with the farmers, who had been his friends — especially as most of their workers were known to my father from living in the village, so that he found recruitment very easy.

The District Organiser of the National Union of Agricultural Workers was a pleasant, middle-aged man called Harry Pearson. He lived in Teston, near Maidstone, and did a conscientious job for the Union. His biggest pleasure was the ceremony of presentation of a cash award secured by his representations to the insurance companies on behalf of members injured in the course of their work. By no stretch of the imagination was he a socialist agitator. He kept very much to the early traditions of the Labour Party and trade unionism.

Although he was pleased to have a new branch in Matfield, Harry Pearson was alarmed by my father's Communist sympathies. They had many arguments in which neither convinced the other. The relationship between Harry Pearson and my father was akin to that in earlier years between the vicar and my father; Harry and the vicar both sought to tone down such uncomfortable enthusiasm for a cause. The vicar, carried in headlong flight along paths where he never would have ventured, now had a quiet life. He may even have regretted the stimulating years when bishops were baited and Matfield parish was always on the agenda at diocesan meetings. But Harry Pearson now had moments of apprehension when opening letters from the Union's General Secretary in case they contained a request for explanation of the extraordinary advocacy of more militant unionism by the Secretary of the Matfield Branch.

31 – BOOKS

Boys' war books – girls' growing-up books – books on British birds – books on wild flowers – political messages.

My father sometimes had pangs of conscience about the money he spent on books, but my mother would always reassure him:

'You've had to give up so much,' she said, 'Why shouldn't you buy all the books you want.'

I can never remember a time when I didn't read prolifically. I had read volumes of fairy stories before I went to St Clair, and was enthralled by G. A. Henty. I lived in the Boxer risings, the Zulu Wars, had been roused to patriotic fervour by his spell-binding tales. My father had shelves of the Nelson classics which were originally sold for 2 shillings each. He had a complete collection of Stevenson, of Balzac, of Hardy, of Mary Webb, of Kipling, of course, because in my father's day he was almost required reading in schools. There were shelves upon shelves of volumes of poetry, including all the works of the war poets. By the time I was 16 I had read many of them.

My mother had a book-case in the drawing room with her small collection of books from her Edwardian girlhood. Crushed among them was Marie Stopes' *Married Love* which saved me the embarrassment of asking her the facts of life. There was a wide difference between my mother and father in their willingness to discuss anything to do with sex. My mother was reticent to the point of prudishness while my father, who prided himself on his modernity, was far too explicit, perhaps naturally in a doctor. I simply could not bear any intrusion into my private world of growing up; I much preferred the veil of secrecy over sexual matters which there had been in his boyhood and which he thought his children should be spared by frank discussion and explanation.

Besides Marie Stopes there was a little leather-bound book, published I think by an insurance company, called *From Bud to*

164

Blossom. I devoured this and found it infinitely more acceptable than Marie Stopes. There was a poem in it about the joy and danger of motherhood which impressed me greatly. I can still remember one line:

> She faced a death by torture, for each life
> Beneath her breast.

This seemed to me very beautiful and awe-inspiring, although I remember hoping that Mrs Hogg, next door, who was expecting her first baby and had spent nearly the whole nine months in bed, would not be called upon to suffer such a fate.

Roland Green's suggestion of several years that my father should write about birds had been acted upon successfully. He found that he could combine meticulous accuracy in description of birds, their habits and habitats with a simplicity of writing he had not known he possessed. He was fluent in describing the beauty of the countryside he loved. Roland Green readily agreed to provide the illustrations for the text of a series on British birds.

British Birds was published in the form of small books or pamphlets: *Rooks, Crows and Jackdaws*, followed by *Magpies and Jays*, and then *Starlings, Thrushes and Blackbirds* and so, through twenty-seven sections, to cover all the birds in Britain. It was then brought out as a complete work by Adam and Charles Black.

This was the lyrical dedication; it shows his ideological romanticising of the ordinary people without using a neutral book on nature to convey his political hopes:

> To the men and women who work in our fields,
> tending the crops and livestock that we may be fed.
> By their work in all weathers throughout the year
> they shape and make the countryside the pleasant
> land that is our delight. Down the ages their skilful
> hands have changed its appearance when the need
> arose, and they will change it in the future. The tidy
> fields are their monument and in our countryside is
> written their history.

Curiously, success in writing about birds, finding that there was a market for his work, did not delight my father as much as might have been expected after his blighted hopes in writing a novel and short stories. He wanted, he told my mother, to write to mould opinion for the general good. He found writing about birds easy. But to relate his descriptive writing, highly praised though he knew it was, to the struggle to achieve a world in which men could live their lives in peace and plenty, was hardly possible.

Nevertheless, he next embarked on a series commissioned by Ward, Lock of six small books about British wild flowers: *Flowers of Meadow-banks and Ditches*; *Woodland Flowers*; *Primroses, Cowslips, Pansies and Peas*; *Cornfield Flowers*; *Fragrant Flowers*; *Roses, Pinks and Bellflowers*. Although my father complained that the artist who illustrated them was more concerned to make pretty pictures than to draw the flowers in the detail he wished, the critics praised the books:

'Rarely in books of this nature', said one, 'is the writing so delightful . . . There is evidence of a wealth of observation and study of the most original character on the part of the author.'

The effortless way in which, as it seemed, he could share his knowledge and delight in nature with his readers was soon rewarded with a stream of 'fan mail' which continued until the end of his life. He tried to answer all letters, using a typewriter anchored to the table with a leather strap so that it didn't shift when he thumped the keyboard with the fingers of his good hand.

One day, he had a letter from an old regimental friend:

Your charming bird book has just reached me and I have read it from cover to cover with great enjoyment. I have been in bed with a misbehaving heart and couldn't attend the Chyebassa* dinner.

---

*The Chyebassa was the troopship that took my father's brigade to France in the British Expeditionary Force, November 1914. Every year they had a reunion dinner. My father always attended with the other survivors, less than half of the original company.

166

His old ornithologist friend, Miss Turner, wrote from Cambridge:

I like your book very much and am touched by the introduction. All the best to all of you.

Reginald Winder, the owner of The Camp and himself a keen bird watcher, wrote:

I must say that you have produced the clearest, simplest and most interesting essays on the subject that I have read. Your prose has improved out of all knowledge.

There was a letter, too, from Sir Roger Curtis, Bart, H.M. Inspector of Schools, who wrote:

I am very grateful for this book. It should have a very ready sale in schools, just the kind of book required.

Among the letters were, of course, many from bird observers. One such, a Mrs Goddard from Bournemouth, wrote querying my father's pronouncement that a thrush and blackbird had never mated. She had watched a thrush and blackbird building a nest together and, although the eggs resembled thrushes' eggs, the putative father blackbird looked after the mother and young, occasionally sitting on the eggs and bringing worms to the young when they were hatched.

My father did not correct his statement in a later issue of his book, probably because he was unable to verify this unusual case.

After my father's death my sister and I found piles of these letters; so I like to think they must have given him more joy than he acknowledged.

Through his writings he started a correspondence with A. H. Patterson, a Norfolk man, nature writer and skilled artist. Mr Patterson, already old, who lived in Yarmouth, always illustrated his letters with pen and ink sketches, humorously depicting his life as an observer of birds and fish on the Norfolk Broads. My father and mother visited him once in his home and thereafter he always wrote to my father, 'My dear old Braveheart', and ended always 'with kindest wishes to you and to your equally brave little wife'.

Sketch by A. H. Patterson in a letter to Wilfred.

32 – A FAMILY DIVIDED

Adolescent Denis estranged – Anne ill – engineering course uncompleted – inventiveness frustrated – a tutor in Tonbridge – Chelsea Aeronautical College.

All was not going well for Denis. He had started to play truant from Cranbrook School and the Headmaster told my parents that the school would not be able to keep him if he did not show more attention to his work. He made no friends.

The onset of adolescence had made him difficult and perverse both at home and at school. He, as it seemed, deliberately annoyed my father by borrowing his airgun, his binoculars, his tools, and not returning them. This of course made my father angry, and there were many loud quarrels when they shouted at each other. These interludes were deeply distressing to the rest of the family.

The loving relationship which my brother previously had with our parents had changed. I am sure he felt this estrangement. Everything he did to annoy them seemed an effort to restore their former attention to him.

My mother had transferred much of her interest, perhaps even her affection, to Anne, who was constantly ill with bronchitis. She would spend a few weeks at school, catch a cold and have to spend weeks in bed with a cough. She must have been twelve before she grew out of this weakness, so her schooling was constantly interrupted.

My mother was indefatigable when anyone in the house was ill. Anne's bedroom was kept warm with a coal fire, which my mother got up at night to replenish – The Rosery was very cold. Brand's Essence and Friars Balsam were regular orders from Miss Reeves, the Essence to keep up her strength, the Balsam for inhaling.

I was now fourteen. My father found he liked to talk to me about books, even about politics, although I had to hide my lack of interest. The sadness, for Denis, who must have felt himself neglected, was that he shared my father's interest in birds and natural history and should have been a marvellous companion to him. Instead, bitterness grew between them.

Although I was fond of him, I found Denis's behaviour embarrassing whenever I had a friend from school to tea. Denis would never appear, although his presence was obvious from the sudden closing of a door, or a movement behind the big red velour curtain which hung across the hall, separating the kitchen, scullery and semi-basement larder from the rest of the house.

My parents were told when they visited the Cranbrook Headmaster that he and his colleagues considered Denis to be a deeply unhappy boy, still deeply disturbed by the assault three years earlier.

'He is very intelligent, with a creative mind', said the Headmaster, 'but it's all going to seed because he can't or won't concentrate.'

The upshot of this conversation was that at last a sensible decision was taken about Denis. The Headmaster considered that aeronautical engineering was a career for which his ability would suit him. The problem would be for him to reach the standard in two or three years' time required by the Chelsea Aeronautical College, an institution attended by several old boys of Cranbrook School.

A former schoolmaster, gentle and patient, had a tutorial establishment in Tonbridge. It was decided that Denis would start work with Mr Diggens at the end of the holidays.

The arrangement seemed to suit Denis. He no longer played truant and his relationship with my father improved. He did get into Chelsea Aeronautical College but his old restlessness returned when the time came to start his career. He never kept a job for long. This was a tragedy, for a small invention he made went into general use in aircraft, although he never patented it. It showed what he could have done if his life had not been so tragically damaged. He had inherited the inventive flair of the Willetts. If luck had run his way he might also have shown the entrepreneurship that was on both sides of the family.

Daily Worker *in Tunbridge Wells — Frances, a 'Plymouth Sister' — beautiful Mary Clout — fire! — Domestic Servant Trade Union — Victor victorious in bus competition — a week with rich relatives.*

My father had decided to sell *The Daily Worker* on the streets of Tunbridge Wells on Saturday mornings. I think my mother was relieved that it was not Matfield; but my sister and I, at school in Tunbridge Wells, dreaded that some of our friends would hear of it. Indeed my sister had a friend, Rosemary Coles, whose father, Colonel Coles, did hear of it and forbade Rosemary to meet Anne out of school.

My Grandmother Willett dealt with the possible embarrassment in a most admirable way. Her natural arrogance made her assume that her friends would never refer to Wilfred's activities in her presence, and they never dared.

Sometimes on Saturday mornings I would be with my mother in the car both when we dropped him at his selling 'spot' in Camden Road and when we picked him up. I know that my mother's heart must have contracted to see him standing there, leaning on his stick, his copies of *The Daily Worker* thrust into the pocket of his coat, except one which he held in his hand with the stick. Both physically and mentally, it must have an arduous task, for few bought the paper, and then probably only out of pity. But what courage he showed! How admirable the character that never shirked a conceived duty! Never in his whole life did he avoid stretching his capabilities to the limit. Although I could not follow his political beliefs, neither could I withhold my pride in my father.

For many years we had had a maid at The Rosery called Frances, the successor to Mrs Cheeseman. She lived with her aged mother in the tiniest cottage imaginable, on the way to Brenchley, one room up and one down. It was semi-detached; in the other cottage lived Frances's large sister Winnie and her diminutive husband, Raymond. Frances was a member of the Plymouth Brethren. This allegiance presented a problem because their nearest meeting house was in Tunbridge Wells, and the Plymouth Brethren were not allowed to handle money on Sunday. So she had to walk the five miles to Tunbridge Wells along a rural road. My mother was very good at coping with the inconveniences of her religion. Frances developed a possessive love for my mother. She made life easy at The Rosery with her good nature and readiness to prepare our tea when we arrived from school. Plates of thin bread and butter were her speciality.

We lost Frances when she went temporarily to Violet Sassoon while we were on holiday. She transferred her affection to Violet. Although everything was done to persuade her to return to The Rosery, she remained at Hatherleigh.

After Frances left, Mary Clout came to us from a large and poor family in Pembury. She was a beautiful, small and frail girl, with a sweet temper. It was obvious that all the household chores Frances had sturdily undertaken were too much for Mary. So helping her with the washing up in the stone flagged scullery, picking the sprouts in the cold winter garden, lighting the fires, were all readily undertaken by all the family. Lighting the fires at The Rosery was difficult before the age of firelighters, especially if the chips were damp, or the logs my father sawed for his wood fire in the study were too green, or the wind blew down the chimney.

We always had paraffin in the house for the lamps and the primus stove, so the dangerous habit of using a little paraffin to get the fire going was surreptitiously begun by my sister and me, when Mary had gone home, which she did around tea-time, and our parents were out. My father had bellows which were fun to use on his wood fire but no use for the coal fire in the drawing room. A most frightening accident took place one evening, when my sister, aged about twelve, threw paraffin on the drawing room fire and was engulfed in flames. She screamed with pain and fright. Between us we beat out the fire which had caught the rug. But she was very badly burned on the arms and hands. After that conflagration, paraffin was forbidden.

It must have been when Mary had been with us about a year that my father conceived the idea of a Domestic Servant Trade Union. He envisaged that Mary would become the Secretary but fortunately, on this occasion, he did listen to my mother, who pointed out that Mary's family would object to her involvement.

Moreover, the village, which had settled down to acceptance of my father's (as they thought) eccentric views, would really be up in arms if attempts were made to recruit maids from The Vicarage, Matfield Court, Friars and so on. Moreover, my grandmother, who had mellowed to the extent of making occasional money presents unasked, would go quite mad and undoubtedly cut off her vital allowance if either of her maids heard about it or those of any of her friends in Tunbridge Wells.

For our journeys to school Anne and I now used the Victor Bus Company instead of the Maidstone and District, which had bought up the Redcar and Autocar. The Victor ran from Castle Hill, near Brenchley, the site of the Aircraft Beacon, to Tunbridge Wells.

The Victors were small brown buses. The driver, who also collected the money, had no cubicle separating him from the passengers. Indeed, his fiancée, a large jolly girl occupied the seat directly behind him and when she got out in Pembury, where she worked, they would embrace fondly and the driver would see her across the road.

There were four rows of double seats on each side of the aisle, and right at the back of the bus two single seats on either side. On one of the buses the springs had given way on the back of the last double seat, so if large passengers leaned back the passenger in the small seat behind could be crushed (uncomfortable, if not fatal). The passengers on the bus were mostly school children. The girls were going to Tunbridge Wells County School and the boys to Skinners School, having won county scholarships at the age of twelve.

My sister and I were the only private school pupils and had to endure some teasing. One of the boys (whom my sister married some years later), was particularly annoying. He sometimes made loud remarks about 'those stuck-up Willett girls'. We, of course, maintained a dignified silence. If one of us sat in the small seat at the back, he would make a point of sitting in the seat in front and leaning back. Probably it was he who broke the springs. Another diversion was to lean over us and bang our window down so that, in winter, the whole bus was exposed to icy air. This sabotage usually led to the driver denouncing him, much to the mirth of the other passengers, especially his victims.

Yet the disadvantages of the Victor bus were far outweighed by its advantages. The driver would stop the bus outside our gate and wait for us, so there was never a chance we would miss it. He did this personal service for all the regular passengers but, fortunately for his timetable, we seemed to be the only ones who were never ready: he would wait while we rushed down the path with unbuttoned coats, books hastily crammed into bulging attaché cases.

On the way home, again in the Victor bus, we would be driven into the Victor garage in Pembury for petrol. This was also the driver's break for tea. The passengers never complained as we all sat in the bus waiting for the driver to re-appear. I usually started to do my homework, the top of my attaché case being a convenient desk — private school pupils did not have satchels.

Anne and I were invited to spend a week during the Summer holidays of 1934 with the Finnises, the well-off family of my mother's sister Vi. As usual they had rented a preparatory school in Broadstairs for the month of August, moving there with their London house staff of nurses and maids.

I delighted in this week, for it was another world. Fuller's walnut cake, sent down from London, instead of Ovenden's yellowish cherry cake; a maid drawing the bedroom curtain in the morning and laying out my clean underwear and newly polished shoes; Aunti Vi and Uncle Leslie dressing for dinner; marvellous games in the school gym; a free run of the books in the school library.

The weather was fine and warm all of this August week. Every afternoon we played crocquet and tennis while Auntie Vi and Uncle Leslie reclined in deck chairs which had footrests and shades over their heads. At four o'clock a gardener would spread out rugs and we would gather round for tea, set out by two maids on a table spread with a white cloth. It was, indeed, another world!

My mother could not understand my insistence that only my school cotton dresses should be packed for the holiday and not the much nicer dresses we had had passed down to us from the Finnis and other cousins. I suppose the Finnis maids knew we were the poor relations, but I didn't want it made more plain by wearing Rosemary's dresses.

Much though I revelled in the unaccustomed luxury, it was not all gloom when it came to an end. Kind though Rosemary meant to be, I felt it a strain to pretend to be more sophisticated than I was, having visited London only twice in my life. My experience of shopping in Weekes Department Stores, Tunbridge Wells, could not be compared with Rosemary's intimate knowledge of Harrods.

Swallow feeding young

Running down – the British Legion – the NUAW –
the War Pensions' Service – Party worker and Eileen –
Daily Worker *nature articles – a missed wedding –*
Tonbridge Trades Council – chauffeurring.

As the years passed into the middle thirties, life at The Rosery
fell into a different pattern. My father had less time for the
garden, so he no longer laboured over the flower beds. Weeds
grew everywhere, except in the vegetable garden, which he
always kept tidy. The front lawn was mowed by my mother, and
my sister and I did the tennis court, for, now in our early 'teens',
we had begun to ask our friends to tennis parties.

As my father sat in the armchair by his study window, he
thought perhaps he preferred the view of wild profusion of
overgrown shrubs, that the birds would sometimes nest in, to the
orderly beds he had once admired, the herbacious borders with
the Canterbury bells, the lupins, the delphiniums, he had grown
so skilfully.

His activities now fell into three compartments. They all
caused the large table in his study to disappear under piles of
papers which no-one must ever move, unlikely though it was
that anyone would ever try to tidy them since only he knew the
order they lay in.

As important as ever to him was the work he did for the
disabled, both through the British Legion, the National Union of
Agricultural Workers and later through his appointment to the
War Pensioners' Welfare Service of the Ministry of Pensions.

Second, his 'Party' work was the sale of *The Daily Worker*
and attending meetings arranged by 'Gil' Bradbury, the Kent
Organiser of the Communist Party. My mother, who got on well
with Harry Pearson, liked and was liked by many of the people,
strangely assorted, who now knocked on the front door asking to
see 'Wilfred'. But she did not like Gil. She once appealed to him

176

to lessen his demands on Wilfred, explaining that, because of his head wound, the doctors had warned her against allowing him to become tired, particularly now that he was no longer a very young man and has recently taken to using irons and a heavy boot to take the strain off his paralysed leg. Gil replied that the needs of the Party came before the difficulties of any individual. My mother never forgave him.

Thirdly, he had started to write a weekly nature article for *The Daily Worker*. He was now recognised as a distinguished ornithologist, but for *The Daily Worker* he wrote not only about birds but also about flowers, trees, badgers, foxes — all the life of the countryside which he knew well and wrote about so lyrically and accurately. Many people wrote to him about his articles (as they did about his books) and he insisted on answering every letter.

He no longer played bridge; indeed he had no time. So two afternoons a week my mother went to a bridge club in Tunbridge Wells, driving there with Lucy Podmore, who had married the only son of the owner of Moatlands, whose sister had died in the Spanish 'flu.

On these days Mary took my father his tea. Sometimes he would tell her to bring a cup for herself and, as she sat on the plush cushion on the fire surround or fender (several holes were burned in it from flying sparks but my father would not have it moved), she listened respectfully as he explained some of his theories. She often must have been puzzled, for she had left school at fourteen and had never been further than a few miles from her cottage home in a country lane.

My parents' friends in the village, with only a few exceptions, were still friendly, but it was seldom they could either accept or give dinner parties because of the trade union or political meetings my father thought it his duty to attend.

He put his commitment to Party and trade union activities before all else. As I look back to those years, I recall that he was not at my wedding in 1948, because of the Kent Conference of the National Union of Agricultural Workers. I had no resentment that he apparently thought a trade union meeting more important than my wedding — I knew him too well. Typically, he had sacrificed his own wishes, which would have been to be with me on this day, to the duty he owed the Union to be at their Conference.

That my sister and I married at all must have been a surprise to Katie Castle, who, so Violet Sassoon said, had shaken her head at the sadness that no-one would ever want to marry the Willett girls because 'Wilfred's politics were so extreme!' (We were then about 12 and 15.) Violet repeated this conversation to my mother as a good joke, saying that she had advised Katie not to upset herself worrying about such a thing, for, in her experience, young men were more interested in a pretty face than in parents' politics.

A few years later my father was elected Secretary of Tonbridge Trades Council. This job involved considerable administrative and accounting work, but it was evidently much appreciated, for there is now a seat in the grounds of Tonbridge Castle with a plate saying it was 'donated by Tonbridge Trades Council in memory of their Secretary, Wilfred Willett'.

Several times a week my mother would drive my father to meetings in Tonbridge, Maidstone, Tunbridge Wells or even further afield. She would wait for hours for him to emerge while she sat patiently wrapped in her old musquash fur coat in the car with her big aluminium hot water bottle (which we called 'the tank') on her knees.

This faithful and essential service of chauffeurring she gave cheerfully for the rest of her life. He took it for granted, and never considered how tedious the long hours of waiting in the dark must have been for her. She never complained and, in any case, certainly preferred to know that he was safe, carried to and collected from every meeting.

In this way of life, 1937 arrived and I left school.

PART III

War Again, and After

1 – LEADING ON TO WAR

University too expensive – college of journalism – Harper's Bazaar – a South African journal – a new car – from crystal to radio – brass-polishing therapy – working men's pubs – the shadow of another war – Munich – South Africa.

It was an immutable rule at St Clair that no-one should fail the School Certificate. It may have been that one or two girls fought shy of the rigorous programme of work leading to the school's schedule of seven subjects, including maths and Latin, and left before they were put to the test. But it was important for a small private school to show it offered good value for money, and this St Clair did.

School leavers were rewarded with a certificate and the publication of their names in *The Daily Telegraph* – the Oxford and Cambridge Boards results were published, but not those of London. (This was one of the few occasions when Uncle Lewis, now Circulation Manager of *The Daily Telegraph*, sent me a fiver, a huge amount for me in those days).

Although passing the entrance exam to university was part of St Clair tradition, going there was not. The girls' public schools and girls' state grammar schools, which still charged fees to non-scholarship pupils, had moved faster than smaller schools with the feminist tide which had flooded in since the Great War and since Cousin Dolly and others had sold suffragette newspapers outside South Kensington station.

Private schools, like St Clair, usually had a prosperous middle-class clientele which had no tradition of sending girls to university. To take a degree cost parents three years of maintenance and fees. Some parents, mine among them, could not find this money. Others, who could, did not consider it worthwhile because their daughters would marry. The generation of women who had remained unmarried because so many young men had been killed from 1914 to 1918 had now passed into middle age; and boys who had been too young to fight were now grown up. Many parents thought that further education would be wasted on girls. Most girls were expected to take a job until they married, but even in the 'thirties some parents wanted their daughters to stay at home. The idea that boys were worth spending money on after the age of 17 or 18, but girls were not, died hard.

I was luckier than some of my friends, who went to secretarial colleges, because my father, again with a financial sacrifice, sent me to a London college specialising in journalism. It was a year's course but the fees could be spread over two years. He decided he could afford it because he was now receiving royalties from his books.

My first job was with the National Magazine Company in Grosvenor Place. I worked for the Honourable Mrs James Rodney, an American, whose exotic clothes and wonderful scents bowled me over as she erupted through the door of my tiny office. She was the fashion editor of *Harper's Bazaar* and I was her 'slave'. The only writing I ever did was to devise captions to photographs. Usually they were discarded! My other tasks were to make arrangements for her to see designers' house collections and make some sense of her scribbled notes when she returned from these viewings. I booked tables for her and her various lovers at glamorous restaurants. When I was doing nothing else I sorted the huge piles of unread short stories so that they could be returned to the agents. I much enjoyed reading them, hastily pushing my current choice into a drawer if I heard her footsteps on the stairs. My work then was certainly not journalism, but I liked the feeling of being involved in the magazine, if not working 'on' it.

I also discovered it was not difficult to write about fashion, once I became familiar with the language. I wrote several articles on trends in fashion, the information purloined from current issues of *Harper's Bazaar*, and sent them to a journal in South Africa, which unaccountably published them. No doubt the Editor thought they were obtaining the services of a writer on the famous *Harper's Bazaar*. I chose the South African magazine market because my cousin, Betty Radford, Great Uncle Will's granddaughter, was a journalist on *The Cape Times*.

In the two years before the Second World War, I was living at The Rosery and travelling to London every day. I was taken to Tunbridge Wells to catch the 8.19 train by my mother, for the first bus was not until after 8 o'clock. The family car, the old Armstrong Siddeley, had collapsed beyond repair. In its place was a Flying Standard, given to my mother by a new friend who had come to live at Boughton Colemers. The Burmans moved to Tunbridge Wells when Mr Burman died. My mother's generous friend, Mrs Dorothy Wharton, was the daughter of a founder of the Carreras Tobacco Company.

I heard in a roundabout way that she was not pleased when she learned that the car was used to take my father to trade union meetings. But she liked my mother to partner her at bridge and was wise enough not to voice her disapproval to her.

The home-made crystal set had been replaced with a good wireless. The B.B.C. often put on fine orchestras and my father was now able to enjoy classical music without the expense of concert tickets, which he had not been able to afford for many years.

My mother was sometimes driven from the study, where they each had an armchair, into the drawing room, by the high volume on which he insisted on so that he could hear the individual instruments. The room rocked with the loud music. In any event, she did not like Beethoven and Bach. Much though she loved sitting with him before the blazing log fire in the study in the evening she was happier polishing brass in the drawing room. Polishing brass and silver seemed to have therapeutic value for my mother. Often at times of tension she was busy with the Bluebell (a brass cleaner) and a duster.

My father was happier than he had been for some years. He was convinced he had found the key to a world in which everyone would live in prosperity and peace. Materialism and selfishness would vanish as people learned to help one another and were no longer bothered by trying to acquire unnecessary possessions. He now patronised the Wheelwrights Arms and the

181

Walnut Tree, sometimes walking along the 'swingle-swangle' footpath which ran from beside Miss Simpson's cottage to the Brenchley road and the Walnut Tree. There he enjoyed the company of agricultural workers. My mother adapted herself easily to the divided world in which they lived. She remained friendly with the Sassoons and the Castles and others from the big houses in Matfield. She played bridge more often, but never allowed her engagements to interfere with taking or fetching my father to and from meetings.

Even Denis appeared to have settled down and was working at Shorts Aircraft Company at Rochester, driving to and from work in an old sports car. There were fewer road accidents then because cars were much slower. Yet he managed to crash into a ditch at Paddock Wood and appeared in *The Kent and Sussex Courier* beside the wreckage of the car under the caption 'Kent driver's miraculous escape'.

The shadow of a coming war was falling. Yet young people enjoyed life in a frenetic way which must have reminded my mother of her girlhood before the First World War. The songs of her youth, many of them gay romantic lyrics from popular operattas like *The Merry Widow*, had been replaced by equally sentimental favourites from the Fred Astaire and Ginger Rogers movies, like 'Dancing Cheek to Cheek'. Gracie Fields sang 'Smoke Gets in Your Eyes', Jeanette MacDonald warbled about 'One Glorious Morning in May'. These songs set the scene for shy first kisses, clasped hands, heady excitement when groups of boys and girls, dressed in dinner jackets and floor length, off-the-shoulder dance dresses, set out on Saturday night to the sedate dinner dances which were the fashion.

We were all oblivious of the threatening gestures of Hitler and the martial atmosphere in Germany. After the 1938 Munich Agreement I hoped with Neville Chamberlain that there would be 'Peace in our time' because I had fallen in love with a midshipman on the Royal Oak and knew that he would be caught up in fighting if England went to war.

My father was unhappy about the Munich Agreement and thought that the appeasement of Germany was dangerous. His patriotic instincts remained strong: he never saw communism as a threat to Britain but only to the economic system by which it was ruled. But he was in a continuing dilemma because, until Hitler turned against Russia in 1941, the Party line was that it was a 'capitalist' war, *The Daily Worker* continued to arrive by post. He wrote his weekly nature article, weaving into it idealistic sentiments about the wider enjoyment of the countryside when landowners had yielded their acres to the people.

At the same time he became very busy in the garden, sowing vegetables so that if, as he feared, war broke out he would be able to feed not only his own family but some of the villagers as well.

He was worried when I told him early in 1939 that I wanted to accept our South African cousins' invitation to spend a few months with them in Capetown. My cousin wrote that I could help her on a small weekly newspaper she now edited by writing a shopping column. I was eager to accept, and my father did not long resist my enthusiasm. His consent meant that my mother also gave in, although I knew she hated the idea.

I cashed my saving certificates to pay for a return ticket and had six unforgettable months in Capetown until, in September 1939, war was declared.

I was frantic to return to England, the more so because in October, just before my 20th birthday, the Royal Oak was sunk in Scapa Flow and my midshipman friend died with all his shipmates. Our love affair had petered out, but he still wrote to me and I was saddened and shocked by his death. I no longer shared the prevailing mood among young people that war was exciting, a time of adventure. The social round of dances with everyone demanding for the band to play yet again 'Hang out your washing on the Siegfried Line' and 'Run, Rabbit Run' became less amusing, an interlude on the way, perhaps, to death.

I booked a passage on the Windsor Castle, a Union Castle Line ship, in January 1940 and returned to England. The big ship, later converted to carry troops, and torpedoes, was nearly empty. It carried only a hundred or so passengers, most of them navy men, returning from the Simonstown naval base for submarine duty in England. A gun mounted on the deck did not seem to offer us much protection.

Civilians were not allowed near the docks at Southampton

and my mother met me off the boat train at Waterloo. She ran past the ticket barrier and flung her arms around me, her face streaming with tears. She told me that she and my father had thought it possible that the ship might be sunk and they would never see me again. While I was on the Windsor Castle, the Athenia, a passenger ship, had been sunk with considerable loss of life. Although we were still, although not for much longer, in the 'phoney war' period when neither side engaged its land forces, German submarines were active. I knew this and was nervous, but the impulse to return home was stronger than fear.

I found The Rosery had acquired electricity in my absence and that the air raid warden had said the wooden shutters used to cover windows in the First World War were inadequate. My mother had bought yards of 'black-out' material and I helped her cobble them up into curtains so that we could avoid the almost nightly banging on the front door and shouts of 'Light showing, there!'

The air warden's activities became more pertinent in the early summer of 1940 when a bomb fell in the field in front of my father's garden hut, killing eleven sheep and breaking the windows in The Rosery and other houses. Mr Ovenden's plate glass window in the village was cracked.

My father resolutely refused to get out of bed when the air raid siren sounded. My mother, very frightened, sat on the top stair, trembling as she listened to the sound of planes, which always appeared to be flying directly over the house. The Rosery shuddered as the bombs fell and my mother would call, urgently, 'Wilfred, please come down!' But he never did.

He was anxious for the safety of everyone else in the house. He opened up the old well in the backyard and put planks over the floor. There was enough room for a few small chairs. It was an efficient shelter except from a direct hit.

Denis had married, and he and his wife Mollie were living in the house. Mollie had a Kerry Blue dog which she insisted should come into the air raid shelter. Getting this large dog down the ladder was not easy. With Anne and I, Denis and Mollie and the three dogs (our two pekineses, of course, were taken down), there was hardly room for anyone to sit. It was also very damp and cold in the well, and Anne developed a kidney infection.

The Battle of Britain was at its height when my 21st birthday came in October. I had a party and asked, among others, several medical students. Guys Hospital Medical School had been evacuated to Tunbridge Wells. Some of the party guests cycled from Tunbridge Wells and arrived with mud on their clothes. They had jumped into a ditch when they heard the whistle of a falling bomb. It was a very noisy night both inside and outside The Rosery. In the morning we picked up machine gun bullets in the garden.

I was working at Orpington Hospital in the X-ray department and travelled by Greenline bus from Tunbridge Wells to Orpington. Petrol was short and it became impossible for my mother to take me to Tunbridge Wells so I lived at Derwent Lodge with my grandmother during the week. The Flying Standard was placed in Tommy's former stable for 'the duration' − a word much used, more and more grimly as the years went by.

Grandmother still had two maids, elderly now and so not subject to war service. Her Rover car, too, had been laid up and she used taxis to take her to bridge. Routine was still maintained. My breakfast was served on a tray in the 'linen room' at 7.30, and I changed into a long dress to have dinner with Grandmother at 8 o'clock every evening. Sometimes as I sat with Grandmother after dinner, the c-r-u-m-p of bombs falling could be heard; but I welcomed the respite from the terrifying air raids at Orpington when the ominous rise and fall of the siren's wail was often followed quickly by the shaking of the hospital floor as bombs fell nearby. Biggin Hill airfield was close.

No concession to the dangerous times of neatness and order was made at Derwent Lodge. If I put a book down on the table at night, it was always back on the shelf in the evening. I understood how my mother's haphazard ways must have irritated my grandmother. Indeed, I found myself objecting to some of The Rosery ways when I returned there at weekends.

The first casualty among the young men of Matfield occurred when the Newbolds at the Post Office lost their son in the merchant navy. The line between the gentry and the villagers was still rigid but the Newbolds' tragedy was felt by everyone. A bold-faced, black-eyed young man, he had been much admired in his merchant navy blazer at the village sports the year before. The village was gloomy, no-one more so than my father at The Rosery.

Sea Poppy

2 – LOVE AND MARRIAGE

Fred – Rex – war-wife – posting overseas.

In November 1940, Fred Atkinson, whose parents had lived in Matfield for some years, in a bungalow on the Paddock Wood road, wrote to suggest I spend a few days' holiday in Shropshire. He had read English literature at Cambridge and his sympathies were on the left. He had often visited The Rosery during his vacations and discussed politics with my father. After completing his degree he had been drafted into the army and stationed at Wellington in Shropshire.

His sister in Matfield had a Morgan sports car and thought it would be a pleasant respite from the noise of the guns and bombs and nightly air raids on London to drive to Shropshire with me. My friendship with Fred was good for us both until he decided to ask me to marry him. Even if I had been in love with him, which I was not, the thought of marrying someone so politically committed would have scotched the idea. I had seen enough of my father's dedication to a cause to realise that I had not my mother's boundless capacity for self-sacrifice.

Our few days' holiday were a qualified success. Fred was able to join us most evenings for dinner in the village inn where we were staying. He usually brought a friend with him so that we were four.

After our return home I had a letter from Fred's friend, Rex Perrott, asking if I would marry him. 1940 was not a time for leisurely courtship and I had fallen in love at our first meeting. I wrote and asked him if he could get a 48-hour pass. Some days later he arrived at The Rosery and that evening, in the dear familiar drawing room, I agreed to marry him.

We were married on Sunday, 15 December, 1940 in St Luke's Church, Matfield.

The atmosphere of war was favourable to such a hasty marriage, but of course my family was apprehensive. However, everyone liked him, even my grandmother. The approval was total as the next two years passed. He was an armaments officer, a bomb disposal expert. Commissioned in 1941, he rapidly rose to the rank of Major. I had a peripatetic life, following him from posting to posting: Shropshire, Basingstoke, Stoke-on-Trent and, nearer home, West Malling. In between the postings I returned to The Rosery to my old bedroom with the Nellie Argent windowpane and the warm welcome of the family.

Our son was born in Tunbridge Wells in 1942. For his first year he and I were always on the move. Then the blow fell; a posting overseas to an unknown destination.

A telephone call. If I would come to the farm where we had stayed in Shropshire for Christmas 1940, he could see me to say goodbye.

I went to the farm. There was a message to say I should meet him at the gates of the army camp, three miles away. I borrowed a bicycle and met him cycling towards me. He had no time at all, he said. The draft was assembling for departure. In that green and leafy lane, our bicycles leaning against the field gate, we said good-bye. It was 28 years since a similar scene took place between Wilfred and Eileen at Crowborough. Every month, or every day, of every year since, my father had hoped that such an agonised farewell would never happen again, and perhaps especially not for one of his own children.

3 – THE TELEGRAM

Mary Clout – buzz-bombs – Morrison shelter – Rex –
V.E. Day – V.J. Day – Wilfred a Labour candidate.

Anne had married a medical student when she was 18 and
her baby, Elizabeth, was born in Pembury Hospital in 1943.
Now at The Rosery there were two small children, for
Anne's husband had joined the navy as soon as he was
qualified.

We were both lucky to have a home that still seemed to be our
own, so near was our past childhood and so strong the bonds
between us and our parents. Other service wives with children
were not so fortunate, although the Sassoons had given a home
to a pilot's wife and baby. Violet Sassoon's heart was big enough
to comfort and cherish this girl when her husband was killed and
her second child was born.

Mary Clout had married her fiancé, Gerry, and was now
living in London. It had been impossible to find a local successor
and an evacuee with a child seemed a solution to the
shortage of domestic help. The Rosery was not lucky. The first
young woman had an obstreperous child of three who, among
other misdeeds, flung the silver spoons into the deep rain-water
tank. While my mother was considering how she could suggest
the arrangement was not working well, the problem was
solved by a miscarriage. Joyce was taken to Pembury Hospital
and Johnny to a creche. From Pembury she returned to London
declaring that the country was deadly dull and she might as
well be bombed in London as in Matfield. It was true that
Kent was not safe, for the pilotless buzz-bombs had begun and
were shot down by the R.A.F. before they could reach London.
Many of them exploded within a few miles of The Rosery,
fortunately mostly on open ground. People stood, rigid, as
the dramatic silence fell when one of these fiendish engines

stopped. An artist drew a cartoon showing shoppers with ears elongated above their heads — and this spoke louder than words when it was published in *The Daily Telegraph.*

We now had a Morrison shelter in the drawing room. This was a huge cage with a steel table top supposed to be capable of supporting the weight of a house. Into this shelter, every evening, we put Michael and Elizabeth to sleep.

Coal was short, but the huge pile of coal dust which accumulated over the years in the coal shed was found to contain a few precious lumps. My father had a large sieve he had used in the vegetable garden and this proved to be useful in the prospecting for pieces of coal big enough to burn. We took turns in this 'mining', usually emerging blackened but triumphant with enough coal for one evening's warmth.

One morning I took the bus to Maidstone to do some shopping. I returned about one o'clock and was surprised when my mother suggested that, since they had all had lunch, I should have mine in front of the fire in the drawing room. Unusually, it was banked up and blazing. My father came into the room and, glancing at him, I could see he had an unhappy expression. He told me quietly, gripping my hand tightly, that Mrs Newbold herself had brought a War Office telegram that morning. The War Office regretted. . . . Rex was dead.

The next few hours, the next few days, were like a dream. I was there, but I was not there. I had not known how kind were the people of Matfield. Many wrote, one of the most sympathetically worded letters to me came from Miss Selina Storr. I was surrounded by love and thoughtfulness. I tried to respond.

'Time and the hour', Shakespeare wrote, 'run through the roughest day'. They did but, oh, how slowly, and with anguish painful to recall.

V.E. day, then V.J. day, came; the war was over.

I think Rex's death confirmed my father in his determination to spend his remaining years working for the cause he still thought would end all wars. He stood for the parish council as a Labour candidate and won some votes but not enough to get in. He was immensely respected for the work he did for the dis-

190

abled. Today there is a plaque in a 'Cripplecraft' home which reads: 'To the memory of Wilfred Willett, who although severely disabled himself, devoted his life to the service of others'.

Skylark

4 – THE LAST YEARS OF THE ROSERY

My grandmother was now living at the Wellington Hotel, Tunbridge Wells. She had given up Derwent Lodge during the war when her maids retired to live with relatives, and she was unable to replace them. She was now over 80 and in failing health. My mother was very good to her. Grandmother relied on her lengthy visits and told my father repeatedly how fond she now, at last, was of Eileen.

It would have been natural if my mother had had expectations (but I think she did not) that, in her will, Grandmother would recognise this professed affection by making life easier for her daughter-in-law. It was not so. When Grandmother died in 1946 there was not much capital left, for she had been spending it for years. The will divided the money between Wilfred and Lewis after a deduction in Lewis's favour of several thousand pounds representing the cost of Wilfred's education at Cambridge and the London Hospital. All the furniture which had been stored since Derwent Lodge was left to Lewis, probably because my mother was not the best of housekeepers and, as grandmother knew, would not look after her precious tables and chairs. Perhaps none of us regretted this loss, for The Rosery furniture, however shabby it had become, seemed indivisible from The Rosery itself.

Denis and Mollie had left The Rosery during the war and were now divorced. Denis had lived in a bed-sitting room in London for the last two years of the War, bravely enduring the bombs. Aircraft engineering was a reserved occupation.

He married again, more happily, and went to live in Southampton where his two children were born, Mark in 1948 and Claire in 1951. Denis had always liked the books of Richard Jefferies, the 18th-century naturalist and author, and called his children after two of Jefferies' characters. But it seemed that, from his birth, the stars in their courses had not been favourable to him. In 1955 he died after a short illness.

I was the last of the three children to leave The Rosery when I remarried in 1948. We bought a house in Petts Wood, not far from the memorial to Great Uncle Will and near to the Daylight Inn in Station Square. We felt a special affinity with Petts Wood until we moved near Sevenoaks in 1964.

About this time, Nannie returned to The Rosery for a visit without end. My mother now played bridge four afternoons a week at the Club in Tunbridge Wells. Now she did so with a quiet mind because my father was not alone at The Rosery; and Nannie always took him tea at four o'clock.

He did very little work in the garden because the surgical boot and irons supporting his paralysed leg tired him. In any case, his work as Secretary to Tonbridge Trades Council occupied him for a large part of the day, and he was glad to employ a young woman, living nearby at Kippings Cross, as a secretary several evenings a week. He was immensely proud that he had been elected to office in the Trades Council, believing that it was a realisation of his ambition to be accepted as one of the working class. But this was not so, as I learned a few years later at the presentation of the seat in Tonbridge Castle grounds in his memory. 'We loved Wilfred', said one of the Committee, 'he was a splendid secretary, but he was different from us. He understood book-keeping and could write very good letters.'

My life was now ideally happy with a husband I loved and two more children, born in 1951 and 1953. I think that one of the greatest pleasures of my parents' life during the 'fifties was our frequent Sunday visits, usually to lunch and tea. My husband, Arthur, an academic economist and an adherent of classical liberalism, was so fond of my father that he never attempted to introduce a political argument which might upset him. Thus we never talked about the Hungarian uprising in 1956. I believe this invasion intensely disturbed my father, but he could not face the issue of the brutal face of communism having for so many years believed in its benevolence.

I sometimes wonder whether his increasing appetite for classical music, which he had always loved, was a symptom of unease at the practice of communism. He never said so, but it was easy to see how tranquil he was when lost in the beauty of music. He had a magnificent radiogram and bought many records. He liked opera; my mother would drive him to Sadler's Wells and visit her sister Vi in Kensington for a few hours, returning to pick him up.

My son, Michael, and my sister's daughter, Elizabeth, were the grandchildren most loved because they had spent their early childhood at The Rosery. Now they gave my parents pleasure by spending a small part of their school holidays at The Rosery.

My father had an operation on his foot early in 1961. He had been having some pain and difficulty in walking, and the orthopaedic consultant believed he could improve this condition. My mother was very frightened. While he was in hospital, she no longer wanted to play bridge but clung to my sister and me. She couldn't bear to ring the hospital to enquire. One of us always had to do it for her while she sat beside us, her expressive eyes pleading that the news would be good.

He came out of hospital, having made a good recovery. But she was already ill. We didn't tell her she had cancer, and she didn't ask. She died peacefully in my sister's home near Reigate. During the last days of her illness she was frequently unconscious but once she opened her eyes and murmured softly:

'Wilfred, I dreamed we were on the Backs at Cambridge.'

Six weeks later my father died instantly of a brain haemorrhage. He had tried so hard to live without her, but he could not. She was never happy without him, and perhaps her spirit called him.

The Rosery was sold and its name changed to 'Willetts'.

But The Rosery, Matfield, is what it will always be to me.

PART IV

Epilogue — 1983

In 1983, I visited Matfield Church, unchanged it seemed to me since my father had been churchwarden. But in the churchyard now lay Mrs Charles Storr, Mrs Henry Storr, Miss Selina Storr, Miss Eleanor Storr, Miss Muriel Stagg, Mr and and Mrs Gill — their grave, as they had wished, in the corner nearest to their house, 'Boughton Colemers', where I had picked primroses long ago for my mother and baby sister. In the quiet country churchyard, with its lychgates and yew trees, lay many others who had lived in Matfield in my childhood.

Would any little girl wander, as I had done, more than 50 years before, along the paths, between the graves, and read the inscriptions on the stones? Find them as sad or as interesting as I had?

My mother and father were not there. Where their ashes were I had no thought, only remembering that they had died within a few weeks of each other. The echoes of their powerful souls and powerful love are in my soul and all around in the fields, woods and the village where they had spent most of the forty-eight years of their marriage.

Never have I believed more strongly, as I stood in the churchyard that:

'Our echoes roll from soul to soul,
And grow for ever and for ever'.*

My parents, the Storrs, the Sassoons; their echoes mingle with many others and are in the very air as well as in the history of Matfield.

---

*Alfred Lord Tennyson, *The Princess: A Medley*.

Jonathan Smith

In his reminiscence Jonathan Smith relates how he first heard of Wilfred and Eileen and how he came to write their early World War I story.

Wilfred and Eileen originally appeared as a hard-back book published by Hutchinson in 1976. It was republished as a paperback by Coronet Books in 1978 with a Second Impression in 1981.

The radio play by Jonathan Smith based on the book was broadcast by the B.B.C. in 1980. The B.B.C. T.V. 'Love Story', *Wilfred and Eileen*, produced by Colin Shindler and directed by David Green, was first broadcast in 1981 and was repeated in 1983. Wilfred was played by Christopher Guard and Eileen by Judi Bowker.

The television serial has been broadcast in Eire, Finland and Czechoslovakia.

In August 1984 it was shown at the National Film Theatre.

After three years the interest continues: in 1984 *Wilfred and Eileen* was sold by B.B.C. Enterprises for television broadcasting in Portugal and to the U.S.A. Arts and Entertainment Cable Network.

*　　　　*　　　　*

Since 1977 Jonathan Smith has written three more books, three more radio plays and three T.V. plays. He is now writing a novel on an unusual theme though in a familiar English summer setting.

Writing *Wilfred and Eileen*

JONATHAN SMITH

I was born during the Second World War. I grew up listening to stories from my father and uncle about Bomber Command and squadrons and friends who did not come back. Young though I was, the words Spitfire, Operations, Black-Out and Radar developed a special significance, not a glory but a power, almost as much as my father's shiny photographs of planes and air-crews.

It was not until I was about fifteen, though, that I began with some seriousness to read history and study literature. In lessons I spent most of my time on the Tudors and Stuarts — or the Elizabethan lyric poets. But once I had 'discovered' the Great War the period became much the most absorbing. Through the writings of Wilfred Owen, Robert Graves, Isaac Rosenberg and Siegfried Sassoon I saw the world in a different way. I was captivated, overwhelmed with disbelief, yet I knew what they wrote was true, all too true.

In these reactions I was of course quite normal, quite typical. For it is no exaggeration to say that millions of my generation, the children of the Second World War, have been more profoundly influenced by the recorded experiences of those who fought in the earlier Great War. As both a fact and a metaphor the huddled corpses in the trenches have perhaps a more lasting power even than the Hiroshima cloud. Call it 'war as a literary experience' if you like, but it is none the less real. How could we ever feel or think in the same way once we had read scenes with Rosenberg's eye, David Jones's *In Parenthesis* or — as I have recently — the poems and letters of Ivor Gurney?

By 1964 I was a teacher. One 1970 afternoon I was no doubt talking to a Tonbridge School class in much the way of the above paragraphs when a very able pupil, Anthony Seldon, told me a

197

little of his grandparents, Wilfred and Eileen Willett. He told me the outline of their extraordinary lives — would I be interested to know more? — if so his mother would be . . .

In no time I was on the 'phone to Marjorie Seldon.

The next day I was shown photographs, documents, Eileen's 1914 passport, Wilfred's bird books and, most important, Wilfred's long philosophical and political writings. Some of it was fascinating. Some of it, frankly, read like a tract. But in amongst the early faded pages I saw a remarkable and inspiring story. To 'lift out' a short, intensely lived section from Wilfred and Eileen's lives would be a delicate business: 'building up' real people with the liberty of fiction can lead you into trouble. It can cause offence.

But Marjorie encouraged me to write the book. Her family was most co-operative, and I set about the research: visits to Cambridge, where I remember looking at the 1913 May Ball menu in Trinity library; I remember walking round the College, imagining I was a young medical student in love. I read everything I could find of that period — letters, autobiographies, correspondence, history. More even than states of mind, I tried to recover states of feeling.

Closer to home, in Tonbridge, I met old trade unionists who gratefully recalled Wilfred's devoted service to their cause. 'Wilfred', one of them said, leaning forward in his carpet slippers, 'tried to live out the Sermon on the Mount. No one ever inspired me as much as Wilfred.'

Although outside my story this later Wilfred was clearly as remarkable as the young doctor and soldier.

Eventually *Wilfred and Eileen* emerged. Through that book, my radio play and four-part television serial, many millions in Britain and abroad shared their lives in 1914 and 1915. Eileen's astonishing courage and tenacity touched countless hearts. Yet, because of its short time-span and unanswered questions, not all readers and viewers were satisfied. Far from it:

'What happened to Wilfred and Eileen?'

'Did they have children? If so . . .'

'What was Wilfred like after the War?'

'How long did they live?'

Now, with her greater knowledge and intimate insight, Marjorie Seldon has answered these and many more questions. Her support to me was invaluable and I am delighted to see this frank and illuminating book published.

In the course of writing *Wilfred and Eileen* I often regretted I never met them in their lifetime. Having read *Poppies and Roses* I feel I now have.

. . . the next two E & L books

THE NEW RIGHT

Why are Left journals and writers intrigued by 'the new Right'? Why are some contemptuous, but more and more respectful?

Why is 'the new Right' called 'radical'?, 'neo-liberal'? 'libertarian'?

Why is it becoming more discussed than the old Right? Or than the new Left – hard (Marxist, Trotskyist), or soft (Fabian, Labour)?

For 50 years the young have generally turned to the Left. Why are more now turning to the Right?

In this new E & L book young products of British universities and of all social backgrounds, dissatisfied with all the Lefts and Rights of yesterday, say why 'the new Right' has emerged, what it means to them, what they see it meaning for Britain.

THE LIBERAL IMPULSE
Writing for The Free Society
by *Arthur Seldon*

Contents

I *Introduction: the theme*

II *Twelve freedoms*

    i.   Ownership for All – the freedom to be a capitalist (1938)

    ii.   The War Economy – freedom from political power (1940)

    iii. Retailing – the freedom to buy (1946-49)

    iv. Licensing – the freedom to drink (1950's)

    v.   Pensions – the freedom to save (1948, 1957)

    vi. Advertising – the freedom to sell (1959)

    vii. Schooling – the family's freedom to educate its children (1960's)

    viii. Health – the freedom to spend on medical care (1960's)

    ix. Housing – the freedom to choose a home (1960's)

    x.   Public Choice – the freedom to reject government (1978)

    xi. Tax Avoision – the freedom to reject over-taxation (1979)

    xii. The Social Market – the freedom to say No! (1983)

III *The Prospects for Freedom*

*   *   *

Order before publication at special price: E & L Books,
Box 193, Sevenoaks, Kent, TN15 0JW.